W9-DCG-235

Making a Difference in a Globalized World

Making a Difference in a Globalized World

Short-term Missions That Work

Laurie A. Occhipinti

ROWMAN & LITTLEFIELD
Lanham • Boulder • New York • London

Published by Rowman & Littlefield
A wholly owned subsidiary of The Rowman & Littlefield Publishing Group, Inc.
4501 Forbes Boulevard, Suite 200, Lanham, Maryland 20706
www.rowman.com

16 Carlisle Street, London W1D 3BT, United Kingdom

Copyright © 2014 by The Alban Institute

All rights reserved. No part of this book may be reproduced in any form or by any
electronic or mechanical means, including information storage and retrieval systems,
without written permission from the publisher, except by a reviewer who may quote
passages in a review.

British Library Cataloguing in Publication Information Available

Library of Congress Cataloging-in-Publication Data

Occhipinti, Laurie A., 1968–
Making a difference in a globalized world : short-term missions that work / Laurie A. Occhipinti.
pages cm.
Includes bibliographical references.
ISBN 978-1-56699-758-4 (cloth) — ISBN 978-1-56699-443-9 (pbk.) — ISBN 978-1-56699-716-4
(ebook) 1. Short-term missions. I. Title.
BV2082.S56O23 2013
266'.02373—dc23
2013025989

∞™ The paper used in this publication meets the minimum requirements of American
National Standard for Information Sciences Permanence of Paper for Printed Library
Materials, ANSI/NISO Z39.48-1992.

Printed in the United States of America

Contents

Foreword

I have a vivid memory of the first time I met Laurie Occhipinti. Along with twelve other anthropologists, including myself, she was presenting a paper on the topic of short-term mission trips at the American Anthropological Association (AAA). While earlier anthropologists had thought of tourism or short-term missions as trivial phenomena not meriting serious scholarship, tourism research had moved into the center of mainstream anthropological scholarship as an important arena for studying globalization, transnationalism, and cultural change. By contrast, this 2006 double session of the AAA would be the first time that short-term mission trips would receive such anthropological attention.

I had wondered if fellow anthropologists would be primarily critical or dismissive of those doing mission trips, and was pleasantly surprised by the quality and sensitivity of presentations and by the strong interest expressed by attendees. Laurie's paper stood out. She said that many of her students were taking her anthropology classes purely to fulfill a general education requirement, and had little or no interest in peoples and cultures outside the United States. But in recent years she had been encouraged by the growing presence of students who expressed deep interest in the cultures she described. When she spoke with these students privately, many told her that their interest in other peoples and cultures came from having traveled on church mission trips to the very places and cultures focused on in her teaching. She learned that while many of her students were using spring break to head to the beaches of Tijuana to party, others were heading to the slums of Tijuana on mission trips to work with the poor. And it was the second group which was more responsive to her anthropological focus on other peoples. When she saw my call for papers in the anthropology of religion listserve, Laurie immediately decided to interview her students about how they were using their spring break. Her resulting AAA paper was fascinating, and much appreciated by all. A few months later (in March of 2007) Laurie joined a small group of scholars for a three-day research colloquium on this topic, co-led by Robert Wuthnow and myself, where we reviewed Wuthnow's national random data showing that 1.6 million US adults traveled abroad each year on mission trips, and where we brainstormed research plans related to short-term missions. Could we help organize a community of scholars focusing on this topic, just as anthropologists had already done with tourism? After six years, and a great deal more research, Laurie is now sharing the results of her research with us all.

While there are many books about short-term missions that are written at a popular level and are not grounded in research, this book represents the front edge of a gradually emerging set of research-based writings on mission trips. But while most of what has been written on this topic by scholars appears in the form of journal articles or chapters in edited books, this book is one of only two or three single-author books wholly focused on this topic that are grounded in research. And it combines a number of unusual strengths.

First, while much of the research on short-term missions relies on the memories and understandings of mission trip participants to report information (using questionnaires or interviews), Occhipinti uses participant-observation with a congregation in Ohio and accompanied the congregational members on mission trips to the Dominican Republic. Because of her fluency in Spanish, she served as a team translator, thus gaining firsthand observation of intercultural communications and dynamics involved. That is, she not only has done an enormous number of interviews with mission trip participants, but also has made use of firsthand observation to supplement and flesh out what she learned through interviews.

Second, while much of the research on short-term missions is carried out by non-anthropologists and focuses exclusively on the mission trip travelers, with no focus on those being partnered with in destination sites, this research was carried out by an anthropologist fluent in Spanish, with many years of experience in Latin America, and with a clear focus on the actual relationships being forged across language and culture and socioeconomic level.

Third, this book accurately recognizes that the majority of mission trips involve partnership activities across major socioeconomic divides and where issues related to human poverty are central. Mission teams are not primarily going from places where there are Christians and churches to places where there are not, but are rather going to places where they are partnering with local Christians and local churches in projects of various sorts, but where the single biggest difference between the travelers and those they partner with is economic. And because Occhipinti is an expert in development and in economic anthropology, she is able to focus her strengths on what is precisely at the core of most mission trip activities and partnerships.

Finally, rather than writing a highly technical or theoretical book about mission trip participants intended to be read primarily by other academics, she has produced a work of public anthropology, a book intended to be read by the very people she writes about—those who participate in mission trips. She is sympathetic to the goals of mission trip participants, and wonderfully draws from her strengths as an applied anthropologist to help such participants understand the very sorts of things that they themselves will find helpful and practical as they grapple with socioeconomic inequities of our world. No other book does a better job of focusing on partnerships across such divides.

Robert J. Priest
G. W. Aldeen Professor of International Studies
Professor of Mission and Anthropology
Trinity Evangelical Divinity School

Preface

I walked hesitantly into the church sanctuary where I was to meet with the pastor, Ralph Hawkins. I was there to ask him if he and his congregation would be willing to consider letting me accompany them on their next short-term mission trip to the Dominican Republic. On that Friday morning, the sanctuary was quiet and dimly lit. I crossed from the foyer to a lit lobby, open to a balcony above. Couches and a few armchairs were arranged around an area rug. Flags of different countries hung brightly from the balcony railings overhead. "Hello?" I called.

The New Wilmington Presbyterian Church is located in a small rural community in western Pennsylvania. The town itself, spread across low rolling hills, is home to a fair-sized Amish community as well as Westminster College, a small liberal arts school affiliated with the Presbyterian church. The traditional brick church, located on the main street of the town at the edge of the college campus, felt comfortably familiar. On my travel there, I gazed at the landscape, noticing how similar it seemed to New England, where I had grown up, with its trees and hills. But western Pennsylvania was different too, more rural, more open, more isolated.

As I peered around the lobby, a tall man appeared out of one of the doorways around its perimeters. "Laurie?" he called cheerfully. "I'm glad you made it. Come on in."

As we settled into Ralph's office, I began to repeat what I had told him on the phone. I explained that I work as a cultural anthropologist as well as teach at a small public college in a town about an hour from New Wilmington. I expressed an interest in starting a research project focusing on the experiences and perspectives of people participating in short-term mission work. I had a colleague at my university who was a member of the New Wilmington church, and she had enthusiastically suggested that her congregation might be a good place for me to start. Ralph nodded and asked me to tell him more about what my project might entail and what my research background was. Like most researchers, I didn't need a second invitation to talk more about what it is I do.

Since the mid-1990s, I have been studying poverty and economic development in Latin America. In particular, I have worked with faith-based organizations that run antipoverty programs, mostly in rural indigenous communities. I began that project back when nongovernmental organizations (NGOs) were becoming increasingly important in the global efforts to initiate and manage programs to help the poor. I quickly realized that a large number of NGOs were affiliated with religious organizations. I became interested in looking at the relation between religion and antipoverty work and to what extent religious NGOs were different from their secular counterparts. That project took me to northwestern Argentina, where I worked closely with two Catholic organizations. Over the course of that year, I discovered that a faith-based approach did matter, and in significant ways. The organizations I worked with defined the mission to help the poor very broadly. They weren't just trying to alleviate poverty. They were invested in certain ideals—to care for others, yes, but also to promote human dignity and a more just and equitable society. Many secular NGOs have similar secondary aims for their antipoverty work, but for the faith-based NGOs I worked with, those ideals were essential to their understanding and purpose.

As I settled in to teaching university students in western Pennsylvania, I told Ralph, I had finished—or at least, come to a pause in—this research. I now worked with my students, teaching about global cultures and cross-cultural understanding, and so I routinely asked them if they had traveled abroad or had any cross-cultural experiences. Although a few of them mentioned family vacations or study abroad, far more of them said they had visited another country as part of a church group, as short-term missionaries. I wanted to know more about this. I was starting this research with two broad questions. First, how did this experience of traveling abroad as a part of a short-term mission shape the perceptions of the American participants about themselves and their understanding of other cultures? Second, how do short-term missions intersect with the kinds of antipoverty programs I looked at in my earlier research? Many, but not all, short-term missions include a "service" component—some kind of project intended to combat conditions of poverty.

As I continued to explain what I was thinking, Ralph seemed to show a lot of interest. I told him that I had approached the New Wilmington church because it fit certain characteristics that I thought would help me understand the answers to these questions. I wanted to look at a congregation-based program, which so many short-term mission projects are. Because I was interested in the relation of short-term missions to poverty, I wanted to study a group whose project was focused on service rather than evangelism or conversion. I added a few other preferences. I wanted to work with a group comprising mainly adults. Many short-term mission trips are aimed at young adults or teens, and although this is an important part of the landscape of these projects, I had already done a preliminary set of interviews with college student participants. Those interviews suggested that for young adults, an important, perhaps critical, part of a mission trip was a sense of personal transformation. I wanted to see to what extent a short-term mission trip experience was different for older adults, with a wider range of life experiences. I wanted to work with a program that was well established, so that logistical details of the program and individual personalities of participants might play a smaller role. Finally, I wanted to work with a congregation within a mainline denomination, as this fits with my own faith background in ways that I thought would facilitate my relationships within the group. (More on that later.) Last, as I continued to explain to Ralph, although as an anthropologist I do not really deal substantively with issues of theology, I am interested in the ways in which poverty is understood as a moral and religious problem. This was a key issue in my work in Argentina with progressive Catholic organizations that drew much inspiration from liberation theology. I wanted to be able to compare those theological perspectives with what I found within mainline Protestantism.

"Well," Ralph said thoughtfully, "this sounds like an interesting project. But what is it exactly that you are going to *do*? What would your research look like, from our perspective?"

I frequently find myself explaining to people what an anthropologist is and what we do. Even among other academics, my field of study is frequently misunderstood. When I came back from my first trip to the Dominican Republic, a colleague asked, "So, did you dig up anything good?" I often find myself explaining that while some anthropologists—archaeologists—do dig things up, I am interested in living people. Simply put, anthropology is the study of humanity. What distinguishes anthropology from other fields that study people—like sociology or psychology—is mostly approach. Anthropologists take a holistic perspective on culture, focusing on the interrelationships and interconnections between parts of systems. Although surveys, statistics, and other kinds of measurements are useful and helpful, like many cultural anthropologists, I rely more heavily on an in-depth, personal process of collecting information—listening, participating, observing. What I wanted to do was to accompany Ralph's team as they went to the Dominican Republic, to experience a short-term mission for myself. I explained that I would not just be sitting back with a notebook, watching what people were doing and taking notes. I would not just be a wordless observer. Rather, I would be actively participating in the day-to-day experiences, talking to people as we went, in order to better understand what was happening. Ralph asked if I would be willing to pitch in with the work of the team, and I replied that it would be important, almost essential, that I did. We discussed the options for roles on the team and quickly agreed that since I spoke Spanish, a skill that was in rather short supply that year among team members, I would work as an interpreter. This would give me a defined role, allow me to gain a perspective on the work of the team and contribute something to the group. In addition to participating and observing during the trip, I would also ask team members to sit with me for more formal interviews, both while we were in Pennsylvania before and after the trip and during the trip itself when there were opportunities to do so.

I am constantly amazed that anyone agrees to work with an anthropologist such as I. I have been surprised by, and ultimately grateful for, the generosity of the people I have worked with in sharing their time and themselves with me. Research is often an intrusive process, and one fraught with risk. Imagine allowing a researcher to follow you around, observe what you do, become a part of your social and professional networks, ask nosy questions, and then write about your activities and answers. Why do people open up to an anthropologist? In some of my prior research, with remote indigenous communities, people there were pleased to have someone from "outside" listen to their concerns and hoped that I could help to relay some of their problems to the outside world. In addition to concrete results, however, some members of these communities told me they experienced a sense of validation—just because someone had listened to them. I was unsure how different conducting anthropological research might be in North America, where I wasn't an exotic foreign researcher.

As I began interviews in New Wilmington, I found that people were still willing to share their experiences with me. In any interview where I presented myself with a pad and paper, it usually only took a minute or two for the person I talked with to relax and open up. An important part of our human experience, whether we live in western Pennsylvania or northern Argentina, is to find meaning in the things that happen to us in life and how we respond to them. Knowing that someone is really listening to our stories and taking them seriously can be immensely significant.

FAITH AND RESEARCH

A final question came up before I left that first meeting, the question of my own faith background. It was something I had anticipated, as anthropologists who study religion and religious communities confront this on a regular basis. It is a question that I was repeatedly asked by both the North Americans and the Dominicans whom I interacted with. My faith, and the way that I answer this completely legitimate question, matters in several ways.

When a researcher is studying a religious congregation in any cultural or theological setting, his or her personal faith background is bound to shape relationships with the group being studied. I have done research in highland Ecuador, for example, where I worked closely with a traditional shaman, or *yachak*. In one instance, he led a healing ceremony for my students to observe, and we had long discussions on the role of traditional religion and healing in the lives of contemporary indigenous communities there. He certainly did not expect me to share his religious beliefs or conceptions of the universe, nor was he trying to persuade me to accept his principles as my own. Instead, my role was to listen respectfully, to appreciate the wisdom of his beliefs and the ways that they fit into the Andean cultural system past and present, and to learn about that system so I could explain it to others. My engagement in this situation was more intellectual than spiritual, more academic than theological. It did require a certain suspension of disbelief, though, which is important to achieve in any academic study of any religion. I was not there to prove, or disprove, that the large volcanoes that shadow the highland valley are gods or that traditional healing rituals do or do not cure various ailments. My project was to understand the role those beliefs and others play in people's lives and in their relationships with one another, with their cultural identity, and with the natural world.

In other situations, though, this question has taken on a different significance for me and for those I research. In Ecuador, I clearly had not been raised with the tradition of venerating the *pachamama*, the Andean spirit of the earth. There was no need, then, to examine why I wouldn't share that tradition, no possibility that I had rejected it; the differences between me and the *yachak* were culture and geography. Working in North America, with a Protestant congregation, I wanted to interview and study people who had a different set of expectations.

Although my family was not very religious, I attended an Episcopal church throughout my childhood and was confirmed and married in our lovely family parish church. I sang in the choir and was an altar server, and I enjoyed the rituals and rhythms of this fairly traditional but socially liberal congregation. Although I stopped attending the Episcopal church as an adult, this faith background became important in my relationship with another community that I worked with in northwestern Argentina. I spent six months in a small community there with people called Wichí, an indigenous population who were hunters and gatherers well into the twentieth century. I was there to look at the relation between the community and the Catholic aid agency that was working to ameliorate conditions of extreme poverty in the region. The Wichí were not Catholic themselves, nor did people in the community I was in practice any traditional, precolonial religion. The Wichí had adopted the

Anglican faith in the 1930s in response to British missionaries who worked in the region. When I was asked about my religious upbringing and I explained that I had grown up in the Episcopal church, part of the global Anglican church, many in the Wichí community saw me as someone who shared their faith background, as a coreligionist, even though I was very honest that I was not an active church member. This coincidence certainly shaped their acceptance of me into the community and paved the way for a relationship built on trust. In a similar way, the fact that I was raised in a mainline Protestant tradition created a certain degree of shared background and familiarity when I came as a researcher to a Presbyterian church.

A researcher's own faith shapes the research itself—the kinds of questions the researcher asks, as well as the ways the researcher writes about that faith. As I spoke with Ralph, I hastened to reassure him that I was not interested in writing any kind of "exposé" or condemnation of the work that the church was doing in the Dominican Republic. Like most academics studying religion (within the social sciences, at least), I tend to treat religious belief quite seriously, at the very least because without the trust and cooperation of the community that one studies, very little meaningful research can be done at all. Researchers who are not at least sympathetic to religious perspectives are likely to choose some other topic of interest. Some researchers do share the religion of the people they are studying, fostering a valuable insider view that can enrich and deepen the research and the research process. Others, like me, take a perspective that validates the reality of religious experience without necessarily sharing it, a kind of methodological agnosticism. This can lead to a sympathetic and meaningful discussion. Both of these points of view are common among social scientists who study religion, and both can lead to objective, valid research and understanding.

As a researcher, I gravitated toward a professional interest in understanding the religious beliefs and practices of others. During my graduate studies, I opted to focus on faith-based organizations simply because there had been very little research done on them at that point, and graduate students are encouraged to look for a "new" topic. As I pursued this interest, I was constantly impressed with the profound and good work that people of faith were doing in their antipoverty initiatives. I found myself increasingly interested in how people's religious beliefs motivated them to interact with the world and with other people. The idea that poverty is not just a social problem, but a moral problem, resonated deeply with me. Ideas of social justice and social priorities shifted to take center stage in my research and in how I defined what I could contribute as an anthropologist. With this book, I hope to act in some small way to bridge the distance between an academic, economic perspective on poverty and inequality and a humanistic, religious one, bringing the knowledge and experience of one to bear on the other.

So, what is my faith background? My answer is a complex one. I have never described myself as a religious person. At the same time, I have never doubted the reality of the religious experience. I sense a greater presence in the world than what we see, and I think that people have many different understandings of what that higher power could be. I recognize that none of us have all of the answers. There is a commonly used metaphor of faith as a journey—and on this journey, we are all at different places. Like most people, whatever claims to faith they make, I struggle with doubt and with concern about whether the world is the way it should be. In keeping with professional ethics in both my field and my own relationships with the communities I work with, I attempt to represent my own beliefs and my own place in this path as honestly as any of us can.

METHODOLOGY

The research for this book has been its own journey, extending over close to four years and a maturing set of relationships. Even as I write this, I am planning to return to the Dominican Republic with the church group again this spring, and I communicate regularly with some of the team members. Although those stories and experiences won't make it into this book, this ongoing involvement helps to give me a broader sense of the work that is being done and continues to shape how I think about the project.

As I told Ralph, I began this research project because of my interest in my students' experiences with short-term missions. I sent out a mass email at the public university where I work, asking for students who had been on mission trips to contact me for an interview. I wasn't sure what to expect, but immediately I began to receive responses. I met with about thirty students, a few of them more than once, and listened to their experiences. At first, I scheduled a half hour for each interview, but soon found I needed to extend that to an hour or more. After about a week, a colleague asked me how my research was progressing. "During all of the years that I have been doing research," I replied, "I have never had anyone *thank* me for interviewing them, until this week." The students I talked to were eager to share their experiences, to process what they had seen, and to work to place their trips in a broader context.

From this initial project, I moved on to my meeting with Ralph and research with the New Wilmington church. I was able to accompany the team to the Dominican Republic, to a town called Sabaneta de Yásica, for two consecutive years, and to conduct participant observation by working with the group as an interpreter. Going twice was quite useful. On the first trip, as a "new" person, I had a different perspective than I did upon my return, when things and people were more familiar. The second trip allowed me to ask different questions and gain a deeper understanding. The group itself changed; some of my fellow travelers went both years, while others were on only one of the trips. I had the opportunity to interview most of the team members individually, both in Pennsylvania and while we were in Sabaneta.

As a professor who lectures regularly to classrooms full of students, I have gotten used to having what I say written down, but for most people, this is an unusual experience. As an anthropologist conducting interviews, I do not usually work with questionnaires or forms and did not use them in this research. Instead, when I sit down with people to talk to them, I show them an empty sheet of paper. It is empty because I don't ask a preformulated set of questions. I explain that while I have themes and topics I think I want to hear about, I also want to listen to what they think I need to know. I want to understand what they have to say, what they want to tell me. I want to engage in a dialogue, albeit one where I am mostly listening rather than talking. And usually, once the interview starts, the person grows more comfortable, forgets that I am taking notes as quickly as I can, and takes me to places both familiar and unexpected.

In addition to the first set of interviews with students and the extensive research with the team in the Dominican Republic, I conducted an additional set of interviews, with the help of my able student research assistant, Jessica Perrin. We identified and interviewed about twenty-five additional mission participants, all in western Pennsylvania. Most of these were adults, rather than students, although one or two interviews included a parent and teenage or college-age child who had participated in a mission trip together. The goal of these interviews was to gain a sense of a broader range of short-term mission experiences.

ACKNOWLEDGMENTS

I could never have undertaken this work without the cooperation and support of many people. Above all, I express my thanks to the participants in the Sabaneta partnership. Their cooperation, patience, and tolerance made my research possible, but more than that, I thank them for their friendship and fellowship over the past few years, which made my own experience doing this research a delight. I hope this book reflects their wisdom and goodwill. Special thanks are due to Rev. Ralph Hawkins of New Wilmington Presbyterian Church, Rev. Chris Weichman of Clen-Moore Presbyterian Church, and Jo Ella Holman, the regional Presbyterian coordinator in the Caribbean. They all not only welcomed me into the project but also generously read and commented on the manuscript for this book.

I also extend my thanks to the team's partners in the Dominican Republic, the members of the Iglesia Evangélica Dominicana (IED) in Sabaneta de

Yásica, and people in the community there for their warmth and hospitality. Particular thanks go to Rev. Miguel Angel Cancu and his leadership team. I am also grateful to Richard Taylor of Journey into Hope for sharing his insights into the Haitian community in Sabaneta.

Funding for travel and research expenses was generously provided by grants from the Pennsylvania State System of Higher Education and from Clarion University of Pennsylvania. I am grateful for this support and for a sabbatical leave that allowed me to focus on writing this book. Thanks are due to many colleagues at Clarion University who offered support and advice at various stages of this project. Dr. Marité Haynes opened the doors for my involvement in the Sabaneta partnership. Dr. Vincent Spina welcomed me into his weekly Spanish conversation group, reassuring me that I could act as an interpreter. Dr. Susan Prezzano encouraged me to pursue my research interests from my first day at Clarion and generously picked up the slack with many things when I needed to conserve my time. Dr. Elizabeth Duclos-Orsello at Salem State University responded with overwhelming generosity to my request for sources on service learning. I am grateful to my editor at the Alban Institute, Beth Gaede, whose knowledgeable comments and suggestions were tremendously helpful.

Finally, I thank my family and friends in Clarion, in Massachusetts, and elsewhere for their support and encouragement throughout this project. Megan Miller was always a willing sounding board for new ideas. I am especially grateful to Joe Occhipinti, who has helped in more ways than I can express, and to Paul Occhipinti for his patience with my endless writing project, especially when I commandeered his computer for days on end.

Introduction

As the phenomenon of short-term mission has grown, it has attracted increasing scholarly attention. Instead of attempting to review or summarize all of the material that has been published on short-term missions, I am choosing a few examples, including some of the critiques of short-term missions, which raise themes and issues that relate in some ways to those I address in this book. Much of what has been written about short-term missions has come from the perspective of advice and a kind of "how-to" approach. The focus has been not just on logistics and practical considerations but also on how mission relates to Christian education, theology, and practice. Other studies have examined short-term missions as a social and cultural experience. Much less research has been done on its impact on host communities from either a qualitative or quantitative perspective.

A number of quantitative studies and a smaller number of qualitative, ethnographic studies have looked at the impact of short-term missions on participants. In a volume of the journal *Missiology* that focused on short-term missions, leading researchers Robert Priest, Terry Dischinger, Steve Rasmussen, and C. M. Brown offered an excellent summary of the research.[1] This article addresses the impact of short-term missions on long-term missions and the ways that returned participants interact with ethnic minorities "back home." The authors find that although short-term missions may produce immediate improvements in participants' attitudes toward people from other cultures, these changes are not sustained. The authors encourage more research in order to produce a better model for short-term missions. Scholar and youth minister Terry Linhart spent extended time with a student group that went to Ecuador, and he also urges more research, saying:

Despite the diversity of perspectives, opinions, anecdotal observations, and theories regarding short-term mission trips, there remains little that we know about the effects (both on those who go and those who host/receive) from these trips and experiences. Participants continue to report them as significant experiences (Rahn and Linhart 2000), yet researchers have been unable to clearly describe the nature of that significance. [2]

A number of studies have looked at returned short-term missions participants to see if their experience, which so many describe as transformative, really produces specific changes in practices and behaviors at home. These studies have mixed results, with some finding no sustained change and others being more optimistic. Linhart cites studies that "found that people who went on one of their short-term trips increased the amount of time in prayer and giving for missions and had a greater chance of returning on a trip for a longer period of time,"[3] but notes that other studies have found no statistical difference in mission donations between trip participants and nonparticipants. Proponents of short-term missions often say that they expand the work of missionaries abroad, motivate long-term giving, and enhance recruiting to long-term missions. However, a frequently cited study by sociologist Kurt Ver Beek finds that while participants reported positive outcomes from the trip, there was no quantifiable change in measurable things like increased donations or participation in long-term missionary service.[4]

Research that focuses on changes in attitudes also suggests that participants do feel as though they have been transformed through their experience, but this change may not be sustained. Randall Friesen, director of the Mennonite Brethren mission program, for example, studies attitudes of Mennonite short-term mission participants using a questionnaire administered before the trip, immediately afterward, and one year afterward.[5] His study finds that while there is an immediate positive impact on attitudes and beliefs, this impact does not persist. In fact, the average on many measurements of values and beliefs, including both personal spiritual growth and concern toward global issues, after one year is lower than before the experiences, especially for first-time participants. The study looks at various factors and finds that positive attitude changes are related to participating in more pretrip training, spending more time on the mission, receiving family and congregational support, and working as part of a team. Princeton sociologist Robert Wuthnow's study finds that 62 percent of short-term missions participants say the experience was personally transformative, while 92 percent "say it made them more hopeful."[6] Like Friesen, he finds that the strongest effect comes when the trip is accompanied by adequate preparation and reflection.[7]

Studies of nonreligious experiential learning may offer some insights into the ways that participants experience and learn from short-term missions. For example, Robert Rhoads and Julie Neururer, researchers who have done extensive study on service learning, examine what a group of college students gained from a secular service trip to a poor rural community in South Carolina.[8] The researchers' focus was on the ability of community service to develop (1) a clearer understanding of the self; (2) a better understanding of others, across cultural differences; and (3) a clearer understanding of the nature of community. They find that students do develop a stronger sense of all of these things, particularly self and community, but a less strong sense of cultural differences. In terms of participants' personal growth and self-awareness, Rhoads and Neururer find that students acknowledge a stronger sense of "something larger than the self,"[9] as well as feeling that they developed new abilities or a greater sense of self-confidence. The researchers also comment on the students' sense that local residents—whom they were ostensibly serving—"have given so much" to the students themselves. In terms of development of an awareness of others, Rhoads and Neururer comment that some students developed a sense that "*the poor* were more than just *poor*,"[10] seeing the people whom they were working with as individuals and developing a greater awareness of social barriers as a cause of poverty. The authors' conclusion suggests that in serving others, one both gives and receives, and that developing an awareness of this can be an important part of the individual growth of participants. An article on service learning by chaplain and professor of religion Mark Radecke notes that reflection is a critical component of experiential learning, saying, "It is one thing to serve and work alongside the poor. It is quite another to ask why the prosperity of a relative few in the world is predicated upon the existence of a permanent global underclass."[11]

Many critiques of short-term missions consider the ways in which dollars are spent. Compared with other forms of charitable fund-raising, short-term missions have a high cost, with about $1.6 billion spent each year in order to just carry out projects.[12] There is little good "hard" evidence about whether the time and money that Americans spend on short-term missions are well spent. Michael Anthony, a church leader, describes his first short-term mission experience, in which church volunteers dug a section of an irrigation ditch that never ended up being functional. He notes:

> Not all projects are created equal; not all projects are necessary; as volunteers, we had the right to get something of value from the short-term mission experience; some projects are better left to nationals. In this case, we could have just paid a national worker a few dollars a day to dig the ditch and he could have fed his family for months. It was poor use of the nearly one thousand dollars it took to get each of us there.[13]

Anthony may be expressing the frustration of volunteers who want the work they do to make a concrete, lasting improvement in the lives of those they want to help. Robert Wuthnow notes, "Proponents of mission trips concede that these programs often benefit those who go from the United States more than those being assisted in other countries."[14]

Yet Wuthnow's research finds that participants are more likely to have a commitment to cross-cultural ministries and higher rates of giving,[15] although whether this commitment is the cause or the result of their participation is not clear. He acknowledges the concern that short-term missions divert energy from other issues, but he maintains that the "evidence shows no harm in participating and supports the view that those who go abroad are usually more involved in other aspects of congregational and missions activities."[16] Additionally, although the costs are high, Wuthnow notes that this money is unlikely to have been contributed to other programs and even argues that a "focus only on the economics of international service is always too narrow."[17] More important, he says, is the larger influence on participants' hearts and minds—how the individual's worldview and faith are changed. He believes they gain a sense of stewardship and the knowledge that with privilege comes responsibility. "Serving abroad becomes a way of learning about these [cultural] differences, gaining a new perspective . . . and building bridges of understanding and acceptance."[18] But Linhart's study of a student group traveling to Ecuador finds that the students "never engaged many of the deeper social and theological issues that arose on the trip,"[19] in part because of their lack of understanding of the local culture and their own culture. He goes on to argue that "without extending careful support and feedback post-trip, the seeds of mission and service planted in the students' lives during a short-term trip may never mature."[20]

Another approach to understanding the impact of short-term mission on participants is taken by anthropologist Brian Howell, whose thoughtful, well-written ethnography is based on work with a youth group at an evangelical church in Wheaton, Illinois.[21] In his view, short-term missions are a cultural event or ritual in which participants know what to expect and learn to describe their experiences in specific kinds of ways. Howell makes the case that short-term mission participants create a story for themselves and for others to explain and make sense of their experience. This story, or narrative, not only frames their trip in particular kinds of ways but also precludes other ways of interpreting the experience itself. In the group that he studies—and, he argues, more generally in short-term mission as a cultural phenomenon—this narrative tends to focus on individual spiritual growth, but it does not provide a meaningful way to address poverty, inequality, and cultural difference, a shortcoming that I hope this book can, at least in some small way, address.

Short-term missions have become a part of the fabric of our contemporary religious and social landscapes for a number of different reasons, many of which have been outlined by other scholars, researchers, and missiologists. At its heart, though, I believe the phenomenon emerges from a deep search for meaning arising out of a discontent with American culture and postindustrial capitalism. We seem to have a collective desire to do something meaningful in a way that doesn't seem possible in our day-to-day lives. This yearning has come together with cheap and accessible transportation and an awareness of conditions elsewhere in the world, facilitated by media and the immediacy of the news cycle. It emerges from an admirable impulse to help, to give, to sacrifice, for the well-being of others. I have to believe that although individuals participate in short-term missions for an ample and diverse variety of reasons, they want the work they do and the sacrifices they make to be effective, to make a genuine difference, and to create the change that they envision.

This book is not "five easy steps to make short-term missions economically effective." As thousands of organizations and individuals have worked for many years to the end of alleviating poverty can attest, if there are easy solutions, they have not yet been found. But I do hope to point the way to a meaningful conversation that will help individuals, congregations, and organizations involved in this kind of work make what they do work better.

NOTES

1. Robert J. Priest, Terry Dischinger, Steve Rasmussen, and C. M. Brown. "Researching the short-term mission movement." *Missiology* 34, no. 4 (2006): 431–450.
2. Terence D. Linhart. "Planting seeds: The curricular hope of short term mission experiences in youth ministry." *Christian Education Journal* (CEJ) Series 3, no. 2 (2005): 257.
3. Ibid., 258.
4. Kurt Alan Ver Beek. "The impact of short-term missions: A case study of house construction in Honduras after Hurricane Mitch." *Missiology* 34, no. 4 (2006): 477–495.
5. Randall Gary Friesen. *Improving the Long-Term Impact of Short-Term Missions*. Abbotsford, BC: MBMS International, 2004.
6. Robert Wuthnow. *Boundless Faith: The Global Outreach of American Churches*. Berkeley: University of California Press, 2009, 181.
7. Ibid., 182.
8. Robert A. Rhoads and Julie Neururer. "Alternative spring break: Learning through community service." *NASPA Journal* 35, no. 2 (1998): 100–118.
9. Ibid., 106.
10. Ibid., 111, italics in original.
11. Mark Wm. Radecke. "Service-learning and the spiritual formation of college students." *Word & World* 26, no. 3 (2006): 293.
12. Wuthnow, *Boundless Faith*, 180.
13. Michael Anthony, ed. *The Short Term Missions Boom: A Guide to International and Domestic Involvement*. Ada, MI: Baker Publishing Group, 1994, 54.
14. Wuthnow, *Boundless Faith*, 180.
15. Ibid., 181.
16. Ibid., 183.
17. Ibid., 183.
18. Ibid., 187.
19. Linhart, "Planting seeds," 264.
20. Ibid., 266.
21. Brian M. Howell. *Short-Term Mission: An Ethnography of Christian Travel Narrative and Experience*. Downers Grove, IL: IVP Academic, 2012.

Chapter One

Recounting Mission Trips

> One thing that was really neat—people will give up their vacation, the money you spend, in order to do this. Most people didn't even bring their family. And you're paying to do this.
>
> —Beth, college student

Despite their popularity, short-term mission trips have not really been examined as a part of the American social fabric except by scholars of theology and missiology. Short-term mission itself includes a wide diversity of trips, projects, and experiences, as the following stories begin to illustrate. [1]

Cathy is a student at a public university in Pennsylvania. She belongs to a large nondenominational evangelical church and has traveled with its youth group. Her first mission trip took her to southern China for three weeks. She described her experience:

> It was really hot there. For the first two weeks, the project was to teach English at a university there. The director of the English department [in China] loves our group—he invites us to come. A big part of what we do is just hanging out with students. We teach some classes and get to know them. We work on developing a relationship, so that we can share the gospel. After the first two weeks, we traveled around. We visited missionaries in Ching Dao, where they run preschools, then we went to Beijing.

Karen, another college student, went to Matamoras, in northern Mexico, with a group from her small church. She said:

> We did women's ministry. That was things like crafts, and we cooked dinner. They were always cooking for us. Then we also helped the pastor build onto his house, and we built this ginormous sidewalk. We spent four hours a day doing manual labor. I never worked so hard in my life. While we were there, I

got to be really good friends with Arturo. He asked me to be on the construction team, the day after I first worked on the construction team making the
sidewalk, since I worked so hard. So he really wanted me to keep doing it.

Karen made a wry face. "And we got to be friends. We also did door-to-door
evangelism. That was hard, especially since I only had three years of high
school Spanish. I couldn't really speak, but they appreciated if I tried. And
we ran a vacation Bible school every day. I translated to Spanish. I'm going
to go back this January, the first week of spring semester. I'll just miss all of
my classes."

Scott, a middle-aged laborer, described his trip to Nicaragua:

> The village was extremely poor. There were houses made just of garbage bags.
> We worked on the school building. People were trying to educate themselves.
> We also worked on a children's ministry. The church is a nondenominational
> charismatic church, so with the children we focused on the basic gospel story,
> with a puppet show. We also gave them clothes. I guess the main goal was the
> school building. And I also preached at a prison. The place that the program
> was connected with had a lot of short-term people, people who would come in
> and work and then there would be different groups coming in.

Alissa, a young woman from an urban area in Pennsylvania, traveled with
her congregation for a week to Brazil:

> We helped to build a house from the ground up. We also organized activities
> with children, fun activities. Then we did a neighborhood walk, where we
> walked around to sing, visited people's houses, for praise and worship. It was
> different from what you can do in Pittsburgh. It really touched me. We also
> had a clean day, or hygiene day. We passed out flyers, talked about hygiene,
> and set up stations for kids. We had kits for them, with deodorant, toothpaste,
> things like that. And we talked with them at the stations, told them things like
> how important it is to brush your teeth, for health. Then we went to one church
> that was an affiliated church that was just built. It was very interesting to see
> how they did the service, and they sang in Portuguese. Then we went to a
> preschool and toured it. Something that stood out to me was that they had just
> gotten a new water filter, so they finally had clean water.

Laura and John, a professional couple with two teenage children, traveled
to Mexico. For Laura, it was her fifth mission experience, the third outside of
the United States, while it was John's first mission trip. They arranged the
trip through a four-year-old religious organization in Pennsylvania. John
said: "The trip was for two weeks, but only one week was spent on the actual
mission. The first and last three or four days are spent on getting there,
because we traveled by bus. During the day, we stopped at tourist destinations and then traveled at night. This made the trip like a vacation." Laura
described:

For this mission, there were two goals. The first was to put in a large bridge connecting the town to its church. The old bridge had been washed out, and the water could not be crossed without it in the rainy season. This job was primarily left up to the men. We brought a frame for the bridge with us from the US. Over the course of the week, they transferred the frame from the trailer to the river, made cement, and used it to transform it into a bridge. While the men worked on the bridge, the women focused on a vacation Bible school for kids twelve and younger.

The only person on the trip who spoke Spanish was a German foreign exchange student, so she was in charge of reading the children Bible stories and teaching songs. Laura continued: "The other women helped out the best they could, and they also came up with games to teach and crafts to do. In the afternoons, after work was done, a majority of the men would return to town and join in on the activities of the Bible school. There was one pediatrician who gave out medication to the local people, but she worked on her own for the most part."

These stories begin to illustrate some of the range of experiences that people have as part of short-term missions. Visiting unfamiliar places, working with people from different ethnic and class backgrounds, dealing with limited language skills, and sharing religious faith are central to nearly all of the accounts, although the details can be very different.

A HISTORY OF SHORT-TERM MISSION

Christian missions have, of course, a long and complex history. Evangelism itself is built into the very fabric of Christian doctrine and belief. Since the Spanish Conquest, missions played an important role in colonialism, a role that was not just religious but also social and political. Missionaries were often used by colonial governments as a way to change behaviors, extending the cultural norms of the colonial nation into remote regions. Missions functioned as government outposts, extending political control into the countryside. The populations on the "receiving" end of missions often had little choice about religious conversion, at least for the sake of appearances, but in some regions at least, missions were less brutal than outright military conquest. The presence of missions sometimes shielded populations from military conquest, providing a safe haven of sorts. Although missions used native labor, they often provided somewhat more benign working conditions than other colonial institutions.[2] And missions provided critical social services, particularly in education and health care.

During the nineteenth and the early part of the twentieth centuries, missionaries from Europe and the United States served abroad for periods of years, sometimes decades. In most denominations, mission work was seen as a career or vocation, rather than as something that every individual would do. Missionaries lived abroad and learned and spoke the language of the community where they were stationed. Their work was not only religious work—winning converts, teaching about their faith, and supporting church organizations—but also economic and social—building and running schools, providing medical care, and offering social services to the poor.

Financial support for foreign missions came from both congregations and separate "voluntary associations" that were often part of larger denominations. Fund-raising efforts often focused on supporting specific missionaries or specific projects. Through the 1800s, denominations developed institutional structures to raise and allocate money, train missionaries, and receive their reports.[3] By the end of the 1800s, a number of nondenominational and interdenominational agencies sprouted up in addition to the denominational organizations. By the end of World War II, new kinds of nongovernmental organizations (NGOs) emerged. Some NGOs were created as legally separate subsidiaries of religious organizations. Some drew their inspiration from religious principles, even when they were not officially affiliated with a specific religious organization. They tended to focus on economic issues, such as alleviating hunger and poverty, as well as on emergency relief, however, rather than on "mission" work specifically. Such faith-based organizations multiplied in the 1980s and 1990s. All three kinds of organizations still exist: denominational boards, interdenominational agencies, and religious NGOs, and congregations and individuals may work with all or any of them.

The phenomenon of short-term mission emerged in the second half of the twentieth century as a new dimension of missionary work.[4] Until the 1960s, "short-term" mission meant travel of less than one year, and usually participants worked on specific projects to support career missionaries in the field. But beginning in the 1960s, and dramatically increasing by the 1980s and 1990s, mission trips of much shorter duration became increasingly popular. Often aimed at young people and scheduled during school breaks, they were seen as a way to enhance the spiritual growth of teens by exposing them to the challenges faced by those who were less affluent. As their popularity grew, trips for families and for adults became increasingly common.

The expansion of short-term missions is probably due to a number of social forces. Evangelical churches in the United States enjoyed a period of tremendous growth in the 1970s and 1980s, which well-known sociologists Robert Putnam and David Campbell attribute at least in part to the clarity of the evangelical message and their willingness to "stand up for their values"[5] in response to what were seen as the more liberal norms of the 1960s. Evangelical churches, by their very nature, place a strong emphasis on mission work and on the need for each individual—not just "career" missionaries—to spread their faith.

The growth of short-term mission trips coincided with the increasing ease, affordability, reach, and speed of modern transportation. Although taking a trip of several months' duration or longer may seem impossible for most Americans, given the demands and constraints of modern life, of school and work, taking a week or two of vacation time is much easier. And the relative affluence of American society means that many can pay for their own travel or contribute to the travel of others. Since 1993, membership in evangelical Protestantism, including nondenominational churches, has declined from 28 to 24 percent of the U.S. population, nearly level with what it was in 1973.[6] But short-term mission work has continued to grow and has now become a common program not only in evangelical churches but also in mainline Protestant churches and Catholic parishes. In some cases, existing programs and linkages, such as sister-parish arrangements or youth camps, have incorporated elements like week-long service trips that echo the arrangements found in short-term missions.

DEFINING SHORT-TERM MISSIONS

The term *short-term mission* is applied to a diverse range of trips and experiences. Although they all include travel, some are international, while others are to disadvantaged communities within the United States. Some are aimed primarily at evangelism, while others focus on service projects. Participants are also diverse—from teens and young adults to retirees, from the very religious to the casual nonbeliever. They come from different economic, social, and ethnic backgrounds. Rather than developing a strict definition, I find it more helpful to look at some of the ways in which experiences that usually fall under the heading short-term mission can vary.

Length of Time

Although the length of trips seems to be an obvious characteristic of short-term missions, it may not be one of the most important. Missiologists generally consider any trip under one year to be "short term," but the overwhelming majority of short-term missions trips are less than two weeks in length, with most being a week to ten days. No matter how long the trip, short-term mission entails going to a place for a limited period of time, and unlike longer-term mission models, does not require the traveler to speak the language or integrate fully into the usual rhythms and routines of the host community.

Sponsoring Organization

Short-term mission trips can be organized through several different kinds of organizations. Sometimes congregations, particularly large ones, manage all aspects of the short-term mission themselves. Denominations may also run short-term mission experiences that they offer to their member congregations. Other short-term mission experiences are offered through parachurch organizations, which may specialize in short-term missions or offer short-term missions as one of many kinds of programs. Or, a congregation may choose to work through a parachurch organization, for example, to organize a trip for a youth group, in a kind of hybrid.

Service versus Evangelism

The amount of time and energy placed on evangelizing versus providing social services can vary tremendously. Service and evangelism are best understood as endpoints of a continuum rather than as mutually exclusive purposes. On some trips, participants spend much of their time trying to win converts through activities like street theater or door-to-door solicitation. On others, participants are fully immersed in service work and never directly evangelize, sometimes because they are working in a community that is already part of their faith tradition but sometimes because evangelism is specifically not a direct goal of the trip. Even when the emphasis is on service, it may be with a notion that people will be more open to a religious conversion if they are aided by, or even just have a positive experience of, someone identifying as part of a religious community. And many trips that focus on evangelism include a work component of some sort, whether it is running a children's Bible program or working on a construction project at a host church.

Group Composition

Short-term mission programs are often organized for specific groups. Many are for teenagers, some are for college students, and others are family based, with mixed ages. Some programs may be just for pastors or church leaders. Within each of these categories, though, the composition of groups may be surprisingly diverse. I was surprised to find that while many programs are based in congregations, participants frequently join a group in a congregation or even a denomination they do not belong to—sometimes because they have a friend or family member there, but sometimes just because it seems like a good opportunity. Some programs, as discussed earlier, are not based in congregations, and these may routinely draw participants from a wide geographic area and range of backgrounds.

Relationship with a Host Community

Some short-term mission programs are developed in the context of a long-term relationship with a specific host community, church, or organization. In these cases, like the group I travel with, while different people may travel each year, an infrastructure develops that supports longer-term planning and relationships. Other programs may visit a host community just once. Some short-term mission groups may travel to an area just once to work with a career missionary who has a long-term presence in the host community. Parachurch organizations may have a long-term presence in a specific area or create linkages with other organizations, either churches or nonprofits, that do. From the perspective of the traveler, the nature of the relationship with the host community can have a profound impact on their experience, as I will discuss later.

THE NUMBERS

Some of the best wide-scale survey data on short-term missions come from the work of Robert Wuthnow, a Princeton University sociologist. Wuthnow has conducted large surveys of American congregations of every denomination, looking at a wide range of issues.[7] Their engagement in mission work is just one of the dozens of topics that he discusses.

People

About 1.6 million people, 2.1 percent of active church members, have been on a religious mission trip abroad in the past year. Based on his survey, Wuthnow estimates that 20 to 25 percent of the U.S. population has participated in some kind of short-term mission experience at some point in their lifetime.[8] This number is much greater than Americans who study abroad at any educational level or who go on religious pilgrimages. Of those who participate, some are repeat travelers, engaging in many short-term mission experiences, sometimes to the same location and sometimes to a new host community each year. Others go just once or twice. Wuthnow calculates that the time spent on short-term mission adds up to 30,000 person-years annually, about 25 percent as much as professional missionaries. The dollar value of this labor is about $1.1 billion, not including time spent on preparation or travel itself.[9] And behind this very large number of participants, there are even more people who stay at home but who contribute financially, host fund raisers, help with planning, or otherwise contribute to the efforts of family members, their congregation, or others.

Wuthnow estimates that 32 percent of congregations, some 100,000 congregations, sponsor short-term missions annually.[10] Members of these congregations are more likely to see their congregation as part of the global community. Larger congregations are more likely to sponsor short-term missions, and congregations on the West Coast do so more than other regions. [11] Many trips are aimed at teens and young adults; about 3.6 percent of active church members went on a short-term mission during high school. [12] Robert Priest, an anthropologist and missiologist who has studied short-term missions for a number of years, notes that in many churches, leading short-term missions has become a "normal" part of what is expected of youth pastors. [13] Most short-term mission participants, however, according to Wuthnow's survey, are middle aged, middle class, and college educated. Many are motivated by the desire to help others; 98 percent of those surveyed by Wuthnow say that "helping people in need" is at least fairly important to them personally, while 73 percent say it is very important or essential. [14] In addition, 92 percent agree that "people of faith have a moral responsibility to learn about problems in other parts of the world and do what they can to help." [15] Wuthnow notes that leadership is needed "to translate this vague desire into concrete action." [16]

Money

U.S. congregations spend close to $4 billion annually on overseas ministries, both long and short term, which represents about 5 percent of congregations' incoming donations. [17] This amount has grown considerably since the early 1990s and does not include in-kind donations of materials or the enormous amount of time invested by volunteers. [18] It also does not include spending that does not go through congregations, so it excludes parachurch organizations, for example, that people sign up for individually.

The Princeton survey also finds that 76 percent of church members gave an offering in their congregation in the past year to support overseas relief or hunger programs. [19] Larger congregations are more likely to conduct such fund-raising drives. This money is usually passed on to denominational or independent intermediary organizations, [20] which "saves congregations from having to make on-the-spot decisions about where to send donations or how to justify particular programs." [21]

THE SABANETA PARTNERSHIP

In March 2011, I found myself at the New Wilmington church where the group was assembling to head out to the airport in the early predawn hours. The night was cold and icy, and I pitched in with the others, carrying an array of battered suitcases from the church basement to a waiting truck. The luggage contained medications, vitamins, and supplies for the clinics that the team would be staffing. We worked with the convivial cheer that comes from being awake at a time when the world is sleeping. In addition to those traveling, a few spouses and supporters had gathered as well, including several people who had traveled with the team in previous years but weren't coming this time for an array of reasons. As the final suitcase was loaded, everyone headed inside for a brief prayer and goodbye.

I looked around the group standing in a large circle in the church lobby. There were twenty-eight travelers, including four teens. The rest ranged in age from just out of college to well past retirement but were mostly middle-aged adults. They represented several congregations in western Pennsylvania, and there were a few more women than men. A range of occupations was represented, which I knew from preliminary interviews I had conducted. In addition to medical professionals, there were two other college professors, a couple of teachers, a contractor, three pastors, and office workers. One more person, a physical therapist, coming from another state, would join us once we reached Puerto Plata. With sleepy eyes, we tried gamely to put names to faces and piled into vans for the drive to the airport.

Orientation

This early Saturday morning was the first time that the group had really all come together. An orientation meeting in February had covered the logistics and some basic information about the community we were going to, but members of the traveling group were coming from a fairly dispersed geographic area, so not everyone had made it. Those of us who did shared lunch and then moved into a corner of the sanctuary, equipped with a digital projector. After a round of formal introductions, the pastor, Ralph Hawkins, launched into an explanation of the history of the project, some ideas about the ethos of the partnership, and a brief discussion of Dominican culture before turning to trip logistics. A short while later, we filed out into the cold, heading home. Although they came from several congregations, many people already knew one another. And as I learned later, members of the group who had traveled together before kept in touch by Facebook and email, as well as through more traditional connections within each congregation.

A group from western Pennsylvania travels to the Dominican Republic every year. In any given year, only a few participants are "first-timers." Most have been multiple times, and several have been many times. The preparation is thus a kind of "review" for most participants, who have clear ideas about what to expect. I found that during the trip, there is a lot of overt discussion of our roles, the nature of the partnership, and what we are doing. This discussion is sometimes aimed at the first-timers in order to explain what is going on. But it serves a more important purpose, as well as a way to reinforce to everyone—those listening and those explaining—why the team is there and how it positions itself with respect to its Dominican partners.

To Sabaneta

We arrived at the airport, still well before dawn. We milled around as the luggage was sorted out. Each of us had, in addition to our own suitcase, one of the suitcases that had come from the church basement loaded with supplies.

When I first decided to go with this particular group, I had been relieved to learn that they did not wear matching T-shirts to the airport. The person who told me this, the colleague who was my first point of contact with the New Wilmington church, had meant to reassure me—which she did. Anyone who has traveled internationally has encountered large groups of missionaries dressed in bright shirts proclaiming their affiliation. Especially in the weeks around school breaks, I have seen airport terminals with many clusters of short-term mission travelers, in fluorescent orange or green or yellow, sometimes seeming to outnumber families and couples on their way to vacation, businesspeople with briefcases and laptops, and tired folks going to see their families.

We arrived in Puerto Plata hours later and filed through the airport, passing the mariachi band that plays an endless, exuberant loop for arriving passengers. As we milled around waiting for all of the bags, a uniformed man came over and greeted several of us from the team. Someone explained to me that he was a member of the Sabaneta church who worked for customs and that he would facilitate getting the medical supplies through, without the delays and confiscated bags that had been a problem in the past. Dominican officials were particularly concerned that no medications that were past or very near their expiration date were being brought in. Many medical short-term missions groups rely on donations or discounts from pharmaceutical companies, which apparently sometimes "dump" unsellable products. The New Wilmington group, however, purchases all of the medications they carry from regular pharmaceutical suppliers. Although I do not know how often groups bring in expired medications or the degree to which it is a problem, it was clearly a concern of customs officials. Even as we underwent a rather perfunctory check on the rest of our luggage, they did still carefully examine the expiration dates on bottles of pills from each suitcase.

As we passed through customs, a notably tall and thin Dominican man, Pastor Cancu, was waiting on the other side and stepped forward to greet the leaders of the Sabaneta group. Usually just called "Cancu" by the Americans and his Dominican parishioners alike, he has been a key figure in keeping the partnership active and growing for so long. Highly respected in the Sabaneta community, he had recently left the congregation there as a pastor in order to take on a new role as the elected head of the Iglesia Evangélica Dominicana (IED), the partner denomination.[22] The IED began to take shape in the late 1800s and was officially founded in 1922 by North American missionaries from the Presbyterian, Methodist, and United Brethren churches as an ecumenical Protestant church. The group was joined in 1932 by English Wesleyan Methodists and in the 1960s by two Moravian congregations. The IED today is one of the largest Protestant denominations in the Dominican Republic, with about eighty congregations and over 60,000 members. Cancu had made the journey of several hours from the capital to join us in Sabaneta for the week in order to facilitate our visit, taking vacation time to do so. Quiet and dignified, Cancu sets the agenda for each visit, working over the course of the year with the New Wilmington parish leaders to determine what is most needed and what is possible, where resources should be allocated, and what the team members will actually be doing for the week they are there.

During the Week

What the Pennsylvania short-term mission team does during their stay in Sabaneta is varied, revolving around several service projects. The focus is the medical work. The team usually includes several health care professionals—doctors, nurse practitioners, nurses, physical therapists, a pharmacist, sometimes a dentist. Most of them come from the participating congregations, while others come from farther afield, recruited through social and professional networks. Each morning and afternoon, half of the medical staff works in a government clinic across the street from the IED church in Sabaneta, while the others work in "traveling clinics" held in various neighborhoods and communities in the area. The work of the medical team is conducted verbally, without hands-on physical exams beyond blood pressure and temperature checks when needed, the ability to order tests, or extensive medical histories. Privacy, especially in the chapel clinics, is limited to six feet or so of empty space between those being seen and those waiting. Pharmacies are set up in each clinic to fill the prescriptions ordered by the medical staff. Other members of the team work as medical interpreters, providing translation to and from Spanish for each medical provider. Throughout the week, the medical team sees about two hundred patients a day in the clinics and a few additional patients through home visits. "When we started out," one longtime team member explained to me, "it used to be about volume—how many medications we distributed, how many patients we could see in a day. That was how we measured what we were doing. Then, the doctors looked at that, and said, 'What are we doing?'" By limiting the number of patients seen at a clinic, the team was able to leave more of the medications that they carried with them with the public Dominican health clinic for use over a longer period of time. "A sense of balance came in—that has been huge. We switched our processes."

In addition to the medical work, another group of Pennsylvanians conducts a youth program, usually directed at teens. For the week that they are there, the team occupies the parochial school of the IED in Sabaneta, sleeping dormitory style in the classrooms that have been emptied out for them. Although the specific youth programs vary each year, one goal is to provide an alternative activity for at least part of the week. The other important work of the education project is less visible and more ongoing: the Pennsylvania churches provide scholarships for about sixty children to attend the private IED school, as well as about twenty scholarships for graduates attending university. A final group of the participants works on various construction projects around the school and the church, a staple element of most short-term missions. The specific project also varies year to year, but the team usually provides unskilled labor—moving construction materials, mixing and pouring cement, or painting. In 2012 the construction projects included pouring concrete slabs for floors, replacing dirt floors in homes of several families identified by the IED church leaders.

The three groups meet for meals and after dinner in the evening, when they discuss the day's events, count pills for the clinics to dispense, and socialize with Dominican church members in the courtyard of the compound. I spent most of my own time with the team working with the medical staff as an interpreter. The number of team members who speak Spanish varies from year to year, and the medical team gets priority for interpreters.

All three groups—medical, educational, and construction—work in close conjunction with various individuals from the Dominican community. These kinds of work partnerships are sometimes part of short-term missions' efforts, but some short-term mission teams focus on projects in which team members interact primarily with one another or interact with the local community only by providing services. Laboring with their Dominican hosts on these projects is beneficial in many ways and greatly enhances what the American team is able to accomplish. It allows the travelers to develop different kinds of relationships than those that exist between service provider and client. It also places members of the community they visit on a more equal footing with them.

The medical providers hold some of their walk-in clinics in churches and chapels, but others are housed in small neighborhood clinics that are part of the Dominican medical system. There, the Dominican auxiliary staff—nursing assistants and secretaries—organize the lines of patients, run occasional errands, and help manage the flow of work. The team also works with several of the Dominican doctors who usually staff the clinics, both at the primary clinics and at the impromptu "traveling clinics" in the chapels. The American doctors make an effort not just to work with their Dominican counterparts but also to do so in a way that is visible to patients. It is unusual for a mission team in the Dominican Republic to collaborate in this way with the public health system; the partnership in Sabaneta between the church and the public health system may be unique in doing so. Because of this relationship, the public clinic across the street from the IED church is staffed regularly throughout the year by the health service, and Dominican doctors are able to prescribe the medications that are left behind by the American team. These last for months after the team departs but not for the entire year.

In 2012, an IED member, Vanessa, joined the medical team as one of the Dominican doctors. She had just completed her medical training, largely funded by a scholarship program through the Sabaneta partnership. A lovely, outgoing young woman, she was proud to show us her thesis, in which she acknowledged some of the partnership members who had given her particular support and encouragement over many years. Although the other Dominican doctors seemed to welcome the Americans, Vanessa was clearly excited to join the medical team. Like the other Dominican doctors collaborating with the team, she saw her own patients, but over the course of the day, she would come to the American providers with questions about her patients or a specific medication. But equally often, the American medical providers would call her in to ask her advice or opinion.

Although the American medical team members certainly arrived with their own skills and talents, as well as a willingness to provide volunteer care, they recognized that their Dominican counterparts were also skilled professionals. The American doctors also appreciated that the Dominicans were more knowledgeable about things like colloquial terms for illnesses, specific local public health issues, questions about culturally appropriate recommendations for sensitive issues, the histories of specific patients, and other kinds of concerns. The mission team is aware that many patients come to the clinic in order to see the "American doctors," in addition to receiving the free medications that are distributed. The U.S. staff, by visibly supporting the Dominican staff, seen asking their advice, hope to affirm and support the local medical system.

Like the medical team, the travelers who work on projects with youth and in construction also work closely with Dominican partners. The group that works with young people includes a number of the teachers from the school—some of whom are former students of the school itself and beneficiaries of the scholarship program—who serve as interpreters, collaborate on curriculum, and help with organization and programming. The construction crew works under the supervision of a Dominican foreman, who is hired along with a crew of skilled workers for the duration of each project—which is often longer than the week the team is there. The Americans provide unskilled—sometimes very unskilled—labor on tasks like moving construction materials, mixing cement, or painting, while the Dominican workers complete the skilled work.

In my work with the Pennsylvanians who travel to Sabaneta, two elements of their experience stand out as most important. One is building relationships with their Dominican partners. Despite barriers of language and culture, the team members consistently describe the relationships that develop through the trip as its most personally rewarding aspect. The other is helping the poor, serving others. These goals are intertwined. Relationships are built through service, and they are important relationships because of the ways in which they transcend barriers of class and culture. The short-term mission experience itself is built around these two interconnected elements. The next chapter will look more closely at culture and building connections across cultures. From there, I will turn to issues of poverty.

NOTES

1. Throughout the book, I use pseudonyms for people whom I interviewed a single time or had limited contact with.

2. The history of missions during the colonial era is long and complex. An excellent book on this topic is *Of Revelation and Revolution, Volume 1: Christianity, Colonialism, and Consciousness in South Africa* by Jean Comoroff and John L. Comoroff (University of Chicago Press, 1991).

3. Robert Wuthnow. *Boundless Faith: The Global Outreach of American Churches.* Berkeley: University of California Press, 2009, 109–111.

4. Brian Howell offers a detailed history of short-term missions within evangelical churches in his book *Short-Term Mission: An Ethnography of Christian Travel Narrative and Experience* (IVP Academic, 2012).

5. Robert D. Putnam and David E. Campbell. *American Grace: How Religion Divides and Unites Us.* New York: Simon and Schuster, 2010, 113.

6. Ibid., 105.

7. Robert Wuthnow has published numerous books based on his research. *Saving America? Faith-Based Service and the Future of Civil Society.* Princeton, NJ: Princeton University Press, 2004; *Boundless Faith: The Global Outreach of American Churches.* Berkeley: University of California Press, 2009.

8. Wuthnow, *Boundless Faith*, 170–171

9. Ibid., 171.

10. Ibid., 169.

11. Ibid., 170.

12. Ibid., 171.

13. Robert J. Priest, Terry Dischinger, Steve Rasmussen, and C. M. Brown. "Researching the short-term mission movement." *Missiology* 34, no. 4 (2006): 433.

14. Wuthnow, *Boundless Faith*, 178.

15. Ibid., 178.

16. Ibid., 178.

17. Ibid., 24.

18. Ibid., 154.

19. Ibid., 141.

20. Ibid., 142.

21. Ibid., 143.

22. Rev. Cancu's official title is executive secretary.

Chapter Two

Cultural Encounters

Every year, thousands of Americans encounter another culture through short-term mission trips. They eat unfamiliar foods, hear an unfamiliar language, and experience different ways of living. Mission participants gain a new understanding of people who live in different cultures, and, perhaps, start to see what they have in common. A primary goal of short-term mission is to build relationships across cultures. The ideas of culture, and of difference, may themselves start to take on new meanings, as participants reimagine the idea of the "other." At times, it seems as though participants' sense of difference and privilege is unwittingly reinforced, which can create a greater gulf. But alternatively, a sense of fellowship can develop across cultures. This chapter explores the meaning of culture by using examples from the short-term mission experience to examine the ways in which participants understand their own and other cultures.

The Sabaneta partnership links several Presbyterian congregations in western Pennsylvania with a congregation in the Dominican Republic. When the Pennsylvanian group travels to work in Sabaneta each year, they bring thousands of dollars' worth of medications, provide scholarships for students in the Dominican congregation, and purchase construction materials to support a range of projects. This material support is important and shapes the daily activities of the team during their stay on the island. But an equally important focus of the Pennsylvanian partnership is the relationships that are built through their cross-cultural interactions with their hosts. Thinking through the importance of such connections can illuminate what culture is and how it works. This question of definition, I think, is not merely an academic one, of interest only to the anthropologist tagging along with the team. Rather, a better understanding of culture allows a better understanding of those relationships and how to build and maintain them.

THINKING ABOUT CULTURE

These days, the term *culture* gets used quite a lot. People talk about organizational culture, cultural diversity, sensitivity to cultural difference, and cultural transformation. It is part of our social landscape. But on closer examination, what does the term *culture* really refer to? Sometimes, the term is used
to refer to ethnicity, defining a cultural group by its geographic origins and
folk traditions. Other times, it seems to point to a system of rules, spoken or
unspoken, that govern individuals' interactions with others. Short-term mission is, at heart, a cultural encounter, one that seeks to create relationships
between individuals from different places and different backgrounds. In order to understand the interactions between American missionaries and the
recipients of their aid and attention, it is necessary to employ a complex
notion of culture. Short-term mission is not an encounter between two fixed,
homogenous cultural groups, but a dynamic exchange.

There is a saying out there that a fish would be the last creature to
discover water. Being immersed in water, surrounded by it, makes it invisible
and nearly impossible to see. When we are in our own culture, we are like
fish in water. Culture is so much a part of our ordinary experience and it
frames so much of what we do that we rarely notice it. We have a habit of
seeing culture as something that "other" people have—colorful customs,
different habits, unusual ways of thinking. We may find some of these differences pleasant and exotic, and we may think others are wrong or disgusting.
It is when we step beyond the bounds of our own culture that we can really
become aware of it and the ways that it shapes not just our environment, but
who we are and how we react to the world around us.

Anthropologists study culture, past and present. And while there are nearly as many definitions of culture as there are anthropologists, it is generally
agreed that culture consists of beliefs, values, and practices that are learned
and shared in a social group. Anthropologists recognize that culture is evident in what people do and think. Culture is a dynamic process, one that is
always changing, not some*thing* that one "has" or can "lose." It shapes individuals in ways that are sometimes part of their conscious awareness and
sometimes are subconscious. It may be evident in how people talk or hold
their body, in rituals and celebrations, in everyday assumptions about how
others will behave. This definition works, but as we look at it more closely, it
is slippery around the edges.

Culture is learned. Anthropologists generally define this very broadly:
anything that is not genetic can be thought of as part of culture. Even how we
respond to the physical manifestations of our genes can be shaped by culture.
The tone of my skin, for example, may be an inherited, genetic characteristic,
but what it means, to me and to others, depends on cultural attitudes and
beliefs about race and beauty. Most often, we learn our own culture as

children, beginning as infants. We learn to speak the language that we hear around us. We learn what to expect from the people around us, and what they expect from us. Formal education is certainly part of culture, but we absorb so much more from what is around us—family, friends, social encounters, the media. We learn what it means to be a boy or a girl, what foods taste good in the morning, how to work and how to play.

We can also learn a culture as an adult, much like one would learn a second language. Some of this learning might come from books and study, but anyone who has learned a language knows that it is quite different to participate in an unscripted conversation than it is to practice in a workbook. Anthropologists, missionaries, and others who want to learn a culture recognize that it is best to become fully immersed in it—living in the neighborhood, shopping in the stores, eating the foods, sharing the celebrations and rituals, passing the time of day. And in learning a culture, we make mistakes, we misinterpret, we bungle. We hope that our mistakes are minor and do not offend, and we learn from them. Eventually, we may become "fluent" in different cultural contexts, able to navigate even very different cultural settings easily.

Culture is shared. It exists not within one person's head, but also within a social community. Yet it is not homogenous. As a researcher who studies NGOs, I am constantly reminded of the differing perspectives of the many individuals I work with. Different individuals in any community have divergent viewpoints, experiences, opinions, and expertise. This is obviously true in a complex culture like the United States, where we are highly aware of our diversity. It is more accurate to think of the United States as multicultural than as a single culture. Although "multiculturalism" implies different ethnic cultures, other kinds of differences also matter. When I moved from the Boston area to western Pennsylvania, I became highly aware of regional differences, discovering that in my new home I walked too fast, talked too fast, and drove way too fast. But cultural variation is also present in small communities, ones that may appear fairly homogenous from an external perspective. Even in very small, traditional settings, we find that cultural perspectives vary in any number of ways. Women and men, young people and elders, the more outgoing and the more introverted may all have very different views, values, and practices. In the Sabaneta partnership, each of the interacting cultures has a multitude of peoples with distinct views, positions, and interests. Just on the Pennsylvania side, the group includes women and men, pastors and parishioners, individuals who had made the trip multiple times and "first-timers." There are people who have very conservative political views and others who are much more liberal. How can a culture be uniform when it includes individuals with differing, and sometimes conflicting, beliefs and values? This diversity and heterogeneity makes culture challenging to study and to understand, but is an inherent characteristic of any culture.

In a similar vein, cultural identity itself is complex. Each of us belongs to multiple cultures and sees ourselves as having multiple, though related, identities. As anthropologist Edward Sapir pointed out as early as 1932, everyone participates in many cultures. For example, one of the participants that I think of as "Pennsylvanian" is ethnically Cuban, her family having left the island before she was born. She spent much of her childhood living in the Philippines before migrating to Miami and only later to Pennsylvania. Although this is a particularly good example of multiple cultural identities, each participant from the Pennsylvanian group brings an array of cultural affiliations with him or her.

In studying and understanding culture, we need to consider many pieces that make up a whole—politics, family systems, religion, ways of making a living, power and inequality, how children are raised. All of these pieces, and more, are parts of culture and expressions of culture. So with all of these dimensions, how do we best study culture? I give my students an analogy: some biologists are highly specialized, studying a single organism, or even a single type of cell. They may understand that specific topic in enormous depth—and that is a good way to study things. But other biologists who take another approach, an ecosystems approach, are more interested in the relation between the parts, the ways in which they are interrelated, the ways in which systems are interdependent and interconnected. An anthropologist is like a biologist studying ecosystems. This holistic approach is fundamental to how anthropologists approach cultures. They understand that the whole is more than the sum of its parts, that systems are fundamentally interrelated, and that a good way to understand culture is to focus on those interrelationships. This approach can sometimes lead us in unexpected directions. As a graduate student, I focused on economic anthropology—poverty and development, and the economic strategies used in poor households and communities. I spent a year living in rural northwestern Argentina, talking to people and gathering information. I came back to my university and wrote a dissertation that focused mainly on religion—because in the communities that I studied, religion was something that was fundamentally interrelated with poverty, with aid programs, and with what it meant to live a "good life." This holistic approach encourages anthropologists to look at the forest, not just the trees.

At the same time that culture shapes each of us as individuals, we shape the culture that we are part of, through our choices, our beliefs, our behaviors. Culture shapes and constrains our choices, even as our choices shape the culture itself. As noted anthropologist Marshall Sahlins quipped, "Just because what is done is culturally logical does not mean the logic determined that it be done—let alone by whom, when or why—any more than just because what I say is grammatical, grammar caused me to say it."[1] Within the frameworks, ideas, and institutions that surround us, we choose how to express ourselves, how to behave. We choose one church over another, one career over another, a hobby, a favorite band. In the United States, we place a great deal of value on such individuality—but we can also recognize that our culture provides the range of choices, the "menu," that we usually choose from. We choose how to spend our free time and our money.

SHORT-TERM MISSIONS AS A CULTURAL EXPERIENCE

Short-term mission trips have become an item on the menu of cultural choices for Americans. This kind of experience has become commonplace in Protestant churches throughout the United States. Given the tremendous, and apparently growing, popularity of mission trips, they have become one of the most significant ways for Americans to experience other cultures in a meaningful way, one that is not limited to carefully managed tourist destinations. Short-term missions function as a space of cultural encounter. Individuals who participate make a conscious decision to explore the world outside their own familiar experiences, to cross cultural boundaries, and, hopefully, to gain a sense of what the world looks like through a different cultural lens.

Choosing to Serve

What leads certain individuals to choose to participate in what represents, for most people, an expensive and time-consuming project? There is no single answer, just as there is no single explanation for why others do not go. Some participants express a desire to "give something back," to try to "make a difference." Others confess quite frankly that their church and community expected them to participate or they thought a service experience would look good. One college student told me that he believed it would be a good résumé item. Most participants have reflected on more complex motivations. The Sabaneta team members encourage one another to think about their motivations and to do so critically. As one team member, an experienced interpreter for the group, said to a new member, "Everyone is here for different reasons. To be a servant-leader, to change your own life, to change someone else's life."

In interviews with me and in conversations with one another, many of the medical providers mentioned that they find the work they do in the Sabaneta clinics "reminds us why we do what we do." When I pursued this, one of the doctors clarified, "At home, there are always issues with paperwork, with insurance. The phones are always ringing. [In Sabaneta,] you get away from the layers of paperwork that are part of our medical system. You have a three-by-five card that has someone's name, their age, and allergies. And that is it." Some motivations that people offer for their decision to participate in short-term mission are more equivocal. One team member in Sabaneta reflected: "The main reason I came was that I was sick of myself. I was having trouble moving beyond that; I couldn't get out of my funk. It took coming here and disengaging with my home life to appreciate what I had at home." Other participants are even more unsure. At the end of the week, one first-time participant reflected on her experience:

> I don't see myself as a missionary—I am not someone who would do this. . . . I didn't want to come. I had too much anxiety. But [another person] couldn't come, and I came in her place. But I was wondering what my purpose is. I don't have skills—I don't speak Spanish, or have medical skills. . . . I wouldn't want to come back [to Sabaneta] without a purpose. I need to reflect.

Like her, many short-term mission participants may go abroad in this way just once, finding that the trip, although fulfilling in some ways, was not an experience that they would choose to repeat. Others find the experience so rewarding that they decide to go again, either to the same location or elsewhere. Travelers gain a perspective on another culture and on their own. For some, this experience is challenging and difficult, while others enjoy moving through an unfamiliar cultural environment.

Cultural Boundaries

The short-term mission experience is explicitly about crossing cultural boundaries. Discussions of short-term missions and culture often characterize them as an encounter between two cultures. A mission trip, after all, brings together individuals from what would seem to be two, easily distinguishable cultures—in the case of Sabaneta, the Americans and the Dominicans. Differences in language, in history, in standards of living, and so on are readily apparent to participants. Yet since Eric Wolf published *Europe and the People without History* in 1982, anthropologists have recognized, and largely disavowed, an earlier, traditional approach that treated a village or other traditional entity as a self-contained whole. It is worth reiterating here that no village, no community, no culture, exists in isolation.

The meaning of "crossing culture" is not straightforward. I recently attended an academic conference in Montreal, and when I was explaining my project, a colleague from New York City exclaimed, "But the Dominican Republic isn't a different culture at all. You can just cross the street, and it's there!" From food to music to baseball players, North Americans regularly encounter Latin American styles and influences as well as people. I tried to gently explain to this New York City native that in rural western Pennsylvania, the distance seemed much greater than it might in a more cosmopolitan center. Despite my disagreement with his perspective, his objection raises the point that in our increasingly globalized setting, cultural boundaries are ill defined and permeable, like a net—easy to see, but also easy to pass through.

From the Dominican side of things, as in most of the rest of Latin America and, indeed, the rest of the world, America is the elephant in the room. Except in truly remote rural areas, American chain stores and restaurants, music and movies, news and economic trends shape people's daily experiences. Anthropologist Kevin Birth assesses short-term mission encounters from the perspective of the Trinidad community he was working in.[2] After describing the encounters of locals with a short-term mission group from the United States, he notes that while the Americans arrived in Trinidad with little knowledge or understanding of Trinidadian culture, the Trinidadians had been thoroughly exposed to American culture and approached the encounter with a good understanding of their guests. In the Dominican Republic, as in Trinidad and most other places, there simply is not a vast cultural gulf between the hosts and their guests, but a daily familiarity with the "other" culture.

In short-term mission work like the Sabaneta partnership, some aspects of culture are shared. Most prominently, the members of the partnership, both Dominican and American, share in a culture of Christianity. Christianity is a religion, and religion is a part of culture, but because there are also norms, values, practices, and beliefs associated with Christianity, it can be thought of as a cultural system itself. For the Sabaneta mission participants, their shared religion is central to many of their interactions. Along with performing service work, the American travelers participate in numerous religious services during the week that they spend with their Dominican counterparts. Guests and hosts see themselves as united in religion, with a shared history and traditions rooted in a Protestant worldview—a tradition that emphasizes progress, education, and individual responsibility.

Their sense of cultural unity is also rooted in the shared experience of the service activities that take place when the North Americans visit. For one week, the visitors work together with their Dominican partners—with medical personnel, with church leaders, and with skilled Dominican workers who direct the largely unskilled Americans in construction work. Together, they see themselves as reaching out to the larger Sabaneta community, shaped by a common idea of charity central to their shared Protestant faith. Both Americans and Dominican partners contrast this shared religious culture with that of nonbelievers as well as with Catholicism, which is the majority religion in the Dominican community.

A project like the Sabaneta partnership literally brings people from widely geographically dispersed regions together and is an example of the globalized nature of culture. It is made possible by inexpensive and readily available modern transportation; it is facilitated by phone, email, and Facebook communications between Dominican and American participants. These connections, technologies, and movements are levels at which "culture" operates and blur what would seem to be clear boundaries between two separate cultural spheres.

Culture and Power

Within the globalized flow of people and information, certain cultures have more influence than others. A traveler moving around the world is more likely to encounter American fast food, for example, than a Dominican restaurant. American movie stars are more recognizable than their Kenyan counterparts. The Japanese stock market is more influential than that of Thailand. Chinese products are available in every corner store, while those from Ecuador may be hard to come by. This disequilibrium is the result of many factors, among them money and capital, size, and historical context. Inequality shapes the relationships that are created through short-term mission in powerful ways.

The Pennsylvanian church members and leaders I work with are careful to describe their relationship with the Dominican parish they work with as a "partnership." They have chosen this term deliberately and thoughtfully, precisely because it suggests equality and parity. Yet they themselves recognize that this is far from an equal partnership. The material resources they provide, if nothing else, create a profoundly lopsided relationship, one they try to address in part by turning to the Dominican parish leaders as the decision makers about how the resources are deployed in the community.

The experience of short-term mission may help participants understand power dynamics better. A study of seminary students who participated in cross-cultural immersion programs found that nearly three-quarters of them reported that they had a heightened understanding of how power works in the world.[3] Power, like culture, is a complicated concept. At its most basic level, it can be helpful to think of power as the ability to make decisions and the ability to influence the decisions of others. Power can come through force or the threat of force, but it can also come through prestige and influence, through government and political systems, or through relationships. Power is an aspect of every culture. It shapes how decisions are made, who controls and has access to resources, and the processes of influence and pressure.

Poverty may be perpetuated because it benefits those who have more power within a society, or even within global society. Existing social arrangements, including economic and social inequality, work to the benefit of those with power. Within the global system, some people are poor because resources are unevenly distributed, and resources are unevenly distributed because other people benefit from that. Poverty is not an accident but rather a result of these arrangements. Because control of resources is itself a source of power, it is difficult for those without resources to gain enough power to change that distribution. Addressing these issues of power and fairness is challenging for those seeking to give aid to those who have less power.

Yet a strictly economic analysis of power in the Sabaneta partnership would obscure the significance of other dimensions of power in the relationship. In the world of short-term mission, North Americans are almost always the ones going elsewhere. Material resources flow in the same direction, on a one-way street. But there are other kinds of resources and other sources of power and influence. For example, the Dominican parish members are often understood by the Americans as being more devoutly religious than their partners. Even as the North Americans bring material goods, they often think that the recipients of their charity are less focused on wealth in a way that they themselves see as morally superior to their own commercial, materialistic society. The ways in which power is negotiated in this relationship are critical to the work that is done, to the ways in which individuals relate to one another, and to the potential of short-term mission as a viable strategy that can work against poverty and inequality. Recognizing the structures of power that frame short-term mission is key to creating more equitable relationships and to reducing poverty, goals that short-term mission organizers and participants see as central to the relationships they create and the projects they undertake.

Through the experience of short-term mission, participants have an opportunity to explore culture, cultural difference, and the dynamics of what culture means. Although understanding culture may not be a primary goal of most trips, it can help participants to gain a perspective on the experience itself, on their relationships with their hosts, and even on their lives at home. Recognizing cultural differences, not only during a mission trip but also in daily life, enriches the experience of short-term mission. Being a fish out of the water of culture can open up new ways of thinking and being, not just during the mission experience but through a greater understanding of our shared world.

CROSSING CULTURES

In the late 1990s, I was living in an indigenous village in northern Argentina doing research for my graduate thesis. During this time, my husband and I became friends with the local Catholic priest, a Spaniard, about our age, who had been in the community for several years. I have never been to Spain, but I am sure that if I went, I would notice the many cultural differences between that country and my American home. But in that tiny mountain village, we found that we had much in common with the Spanish *padre*, from our tastes in music to our tastes in food. Living in the midst of an Andean culture, our similarities became much more apparent—to us and to our native hosts, who saw us all, collectively, as *gringos*. The cultural boundaries that might have been apparent in a different context became far less important in that one.

One of the most important goals of short-term mission is to forge relationships that cross cultural boundaries, that bring people from different regions together in fellowship. But anthropologist Brian Howell notes that the meaning of "crossing culture" is not straightforward. Team members in his study of short-term mission, when asked about American culture, described negative stereotypes—materialism, shallowness, a sense of alienation from family and community. Yet they tended to see themselves as outside of these negative stereotypes, as individuals trying to lead a more thoughtful, engaged life. In defining American culture and their own relation to it in such a way, it is unclear what they would consider to be their *own* culture.[4] Howell says that in pretrip interviews, participants also had difficulty identifying what Dominican culture is, apart from a general notion of poverty, and when pressed further, had difficulty defining what culture is in general. In some of my interviews, I found that participants defined culture only as a superficial set of qualities—clothing styles or food preferences, for example.

However unclear participants might be about the meaning of culture, the short-term mission experience specifically involves leaving one's home culture and encountering difference. Participants become acutely aware of cultural differences in a way that does not occur when one is just "at home." They have the opportunity to become a fish out of the water. A recent study of cross-cultural experiences for seminary students pointed out that such experiences can inspire reflection, which the study authors define as "the act of deliberately slowing down our habitual meaning-making processes to take a closer look at the experience and our meaning-making framework." They observe that through such reflection, "We open our meaning-making or interpretative framework to revision; all our most dearly held beliefs, biases, conviction, and ways of responding to life may be called into question."[5] As with travel for seminarians, short-term mission can provide the opportunity to question our own cultural frameworks in ways that can be transformative.

Youth minister and scholar Terry Linhart spent extended time with a student group that went to Ecuador and notes that "a significant purpose of the short-term mission trips is to challenge and stretch the participants in their faith, thinking, and values. . . . The exposure to the new culture created disequilibrium as the students tried to understand the cultural differences."[6] The experience provides an opportunity to reflect on culture and on difference. And in so doing, it also provides the means to think more closely about our own cultural framework, to challenge deeply held beliefs and assumptions, to re-evaluate our values and our practices. Chris Weichman, the pastor of the Clen-Moore Church, said to me in an interview: "It's important for our folks to have an experience of a church that is broader than northwestern Pennsylvania, with a different culture, literally a different complexion. There are great joys, and struggles as well." Some of this sense of struggle emerges not just from negotiating an unfamiliar cultural context, but from the mental and emotional exercise of confronting and evaluating one's own cultural frameworks.

Ritual Journeys

Journeying to another culture changes how we think of ourselves. There are many kinds of travelers who visit unfamiliar cultures—missionaries, anthropologists, tourists, pilgrims. The relationships that are developed as part of short-term mission are a key characteristic that separates mission travelers from ordinary tourists. The difference between missionary and tourist can be a thin line and can cause some ambivalence. Both missionary and tourist leave home, travel somewhere exotic, and experience differences. Missionary groups often spend time "seeing the sights" at their destination, and trip organizers are sometimes uneasy about blurring this important boundary. Participants in the Sabaneta trip lodge in the school rather than a hotel specifically so that they are more integrated into the local community and more removed from a tourist experience. Group members often commented on the ways in which they were distinct from tourists, noting that the tourists paid little attention to the local people and their lives and were isolated in the artificial bubbles of resort areas. Unlike tourists, the short-term mission participants expect to see transformations in both themselves and their destination.

Sociologist Nelson Graburn has written a great deal about tourism and the experiences of tourists. He suggests that tourism is best understood "in terms of the *contrasts* between the special period of life spent in tourist travel and the ordinary parts of life spent at home."[7] The tourist seeks to experience something he or she cannot at home and draws contrasts between the tourist destination and home. Graburn suggests that tourism can be analyzed as a kind of ritual experience, as tourists seek meaning in their travels. Individuals may travel for many different reasons, ranging from escape and pleasure to more serious exploration of distant places. In a religious pilgrimage, "the traveler is seeking a very important or 'sacred' experience or place 'out of this world,' a sacred center spiritually more important than anything at home. These 'existential' tourists or pilgrims are on a true exploration."[8]

Participants in short-term mission nearly always feel as though the experience itself is deeply transformative. Lisa DiDesiderio, a woman in her mid-twenties, was one of the members of the Sabaneta team. She came to the Dominican Republic with her mother, a health care provider and team leader who had been on the trip many times. When I asked Lisa in an interview what the experience meant to her, she replied:

It made me realize how big the world is—especially since I am living in such a small area [in western Pennsylvania]. I've traveled before, but it was when I was younger, so it is different. It has been a real motivation for me, that there is so much I can do. I have been stuck in the same rut for so long. It's been a big push forward for me, much more than I thought it would be. I have been going through a lot, but this makes me say, life is good.

A college student who participated in a different mission trip said, "People told me before I went that it would affect me and I said yeah, yeah. But seeing how people live there, in a tin shack, gave me a much bigger picture. I was never out of Clarion county before that." A pastor from yet another church who frequently leads youth group trips commented that he saw significant changes in the youth who went on the trip, not only in their formal presentations at church but also at home. He said that several parents of the teens who went on the trip commented on how different their kids were, more thankful and appreciative, although as "time passed and the memory faded, the appreciation faded as well."

These themes—undergoing personal transformation, experiencing a radically different part of the world, and returning to understand home in a new way—are common threads in the ways that people interpret the short-term mission experience. The very experience of travel is broadening and often casts our ordinary lives in a new light. But the travel associated with mission trips is packed with meaning and significance. Many participants say that before they went, they were looking for an experience that would be more spiritually meaningful than anything at home. Upon return, they believe that their trip was much more meaningful than a simple pleasure trip. These are not just trips, but ritual journeys.

In many ways, mission trips act as a ritual of personal transformation. Like other rituals, travel involves a movement from the mundane world, through a period of preparation, to an interval of sacred time, followed by a return to the mundane. The participant is plunged into an unfamiliar setting, removed from all of his or her normal routines and activities. The trip itself involves hard work, usually physical labor, work that is often unfamiliar and demanding. Often lacking accustomed amenities like hot water or electricity, participants must change familiar and basic habits. Participants feel a powerful sense of dislocation. They find themselves outside of their own culture, often unable to communicate with their hosts, separated from their day-to-day routine and from consumer society. They are not locals, and they are not tourists, but something that is less clearly defined. Through reflection on the experience, they look for an engagement with God.

These trips may engender a sense of mysticism in some people. Mystics in other faith traditions as well as in Christianity have sometimes sought enlightenment in retreat from society, in solitude, in prayer, in meditation. In contrast, the short-term mission experience is an American cultural phenomenon—searching for enlightenment in a business that somehow transcends reflection, a constant doing. Being occupied by radically different activities—not word processing but pouring cement—creates a sense of spiritual engagement through action. By breaking out of everyday routines, participants become more highly aware of their actions and the impacts they have. Reflections on the act of service can prompt a heightened awareness of the relationships between the self and others that may not be as obvious in the mundane, day-to-day activities of American life—getting the laundry done, watching television, going to work or school. The participant then returns home, transformed.

Stereotypes and Distance

In the transformative journey of mission travel, how do the travelers see the people they are interacting with and interpret their culture? The short-term mission experience presents the risk that participants misunderstand cultural difference and perpetuate stereotypes, and, in doing so, further reinforce social inequality. Without an explicit awareness of the role of culture, an issue I introduced above, participants do not necessarily gain a greater sense of cultural understanding and appreciation. "We were the only white people in the midst of a sea of black faces," recounted one short-term mission traveler I interviewed after she participated in a trip to Ghana in western Africa. The image is vivid—and indicative of one of the possible negative consequences of the cultural encounters that are a part of short-term mission. Group members might focus on difference and distance—an undifferentiated "sea of black faces"—and fail to see real people with genuine concerns, individual personalities, and diverse perspectives. On some short-term mission trips, participants have limited interaction with the local community. This may be particularly true if a group focuses on something like a construction project, on which they work as a team without much local participation. In this case, participants spend nearly all of their time with one another, and the focus is there rather than on the local community, with few opportunities to get to know people.

As I was collecting stories of short-term mission experiences, I certainly did hear accounts that reflected a lack of cultural understanding. One college student, Karen, related that during her mission trip to China, her team conducted a "prayer walk" in a Buddhist temple. Entering the temple with her partner, Karen said that she felt uncomfortable, surrounded by images and icons that she did not understand and by Buddhists engaged in prayers near statues. With no background understanding of Buddhism or Buddhist worship, or of Asian imagery and symbolism, Karen concluded that the locals were worshiping demons. She became disturbed and emotional and left the temple in tears. Still deeply unsettled by this experience months later, she had no interest in learning about Buddhism and viewed her emotional distress as proof that she had witnessed some kind of holy war.

In another incident, an older woman who had traveled to Liberia as part of a mission team described how local "witch doctors" would "cause illness and tragedy in the area if they became angry with the local people." Her team, she said, "saved" people from the power of the "witch doctors" by asking people who had physical disabilities "caused by the witch doctors" to step forward to be prayed for and healed by Jesus. She said that she had witnessed miraculous cures but expressed her concern that the witch doctors might return for vengeance. I repeat these stories not to criticize these participants or their responses, but because they illustrate the ways in which a lack of cultural understanding can lead short-term mission participants to conclusions about distant cultures that decrease cultural tolerance, personal interactions, and long-term benefits for both hosts and travelers. Studies have suggested that specifically addressing culture and cultural differences in both orientation and debriefing sessions can help participants to gain a greater sense of cultural tolerance and understanding.[9]

Culture at Home

Of course, participants' stereotypes of the host cultures that they visit during mission trips do not reflect the reality of those cultures. Instead, what they serve to do is to create a sense of difference from home, from American culture, from what is familiar. This helps the traveler to see the contrasts and to reflect on his or her own culture in perhaps a new way.

I met with Robin and Jerry Bruck for an interview at their house. Robin, a teacher, had been to Sabaneta many times, but this was the first year that her husband had been able to go with her. As we sat on their back deck on an unusually warm spring afternoon, they described some of the contrasts that they experienced:

Robin: There are things I miss while I am gone—hot showers [she laughs], real dairy products. But being there for me not only helps me appreciate what I've got here, but . . .

Jerry: It gives you a reality check.

Robin: Is that how I want to put it? I'll go back to school and listen to everyone complain. I think, I'll take you there for one week, and you'll see what you have to complain about.

Jerry: I think about the homes that we worked in, how people live. I try to explain that to people here. People here have *hunting* camps that are better. The houses there are made from scavenged materials. My storage shed [he points to an ordinary 8 × 10 foot garden shed]—that would have four or five people living in that much space. The shed is a way better place. The areas where we did construction, we had to walk in. You just look and say, wow, there's a husband, wife, and five kids living in this space, like that shed, with that many living there. We may think they want more . . .

Robin: They have riches we don't have. I am grateful I get to know them. I am hoping some of that rubs off.

Jerry: I am an engineer, I deal with contractors. I think, we need this or that. What I see as basic needs [for a construction crew]—water, a bathroom. There, we carried our own water, and the bathroom—just wasn't there. What I want is not what they want. What I think they need is not what they need.

Robin: You have to put yourself on the back burner, because you are not home. It is a different place. People are people, but their lives are different from ours.

In contrasting their experiences in the Dominican Republic with their lives at home, the comments of team members frequently resembled those of Robin and Jerry. The idea that Americans are spoiled by their material wealth was a theme that came up in nearly every interview I did. Shortly after her return from her first trip to Sabaneta, one health care provider, Kristen Long, told me:

> All last week, I felt depressed. It was hard to readjust. People are so spoiled in our health care system. People kept coming in and complaining about little things. I compare that to what we saw in [poor neighborhoods around Sabaneta]. There were just shacks, houses made of roofing material. There was sewage overflowing in the road. Then we come back to the United States, and the patients and their families are very spoiled. It is kind of depressing. I had a hard time. I kind of enjoyed it being simpler there.

Another participant said, "After I came home, I felt guilt for letting the water run while I was brushing my teeth. Not an overwhelming guilt, but still, a deep sense of guilt that we take so much for granted."

The idea that the host culture is relatively simple, compared with their own, is common in travelers' accounts of short-term mission experiences, no matter where they actually traveled to. One example is that Americans—often stressed for time and very conscious of the clock—often remark on a more "laid back" atmosphere elsewhere. A traveler to Peru commented:

"Life doesn't always have to be fast paced. Western society always wants to get ahead and be productive. Down there it was different. People weren't concerned with time and everything went slower. It really showed me that sometimes you just need to slow down and really appreciate what's important." Another traveler said: "Nicaraguans are very laid back and never show up to anything on time. Because people were never in a hurry, they were much more willing to sit and talk for a while. This time difference was also nice because, if we asked for five minutes, people would always give us at least ten." A woman who went on a trip to the Amazon said, "Americans and people from other developed countries feel the need to better people's lives in third world countries, but they may actually be better off than we are because they can see what really matters in life." Members of the Sabaneta team discussed how people in the Dominican Republic spend time on the street and on their front porches, interacting with neighbors, and compared it ruefully to their own communities, where they felt this practice has largely been lost. Although sentiment can reflect a kind of nostalgia, [10] it also opens the door to thinking about the possibility that the way that "we" do things is not the only, or best, way.

Authors of other studies note that participants' reflections on U.S. culture tend to be negative, and participants may feel disconnected or even angry. [11] Americans such as those whom Terry Linhart accompanied to Ecuador focused on the impact of wealth and poverty:

> As the students tried to understand what they were seeing, they expected to see people languishing and ill-kept, yet they found people who appeared to be content, joyful and loving. For the students these people seemed to be living an authentic life free from the spectacle of *having* that their own American culture valued. [12]

Although the students often misinterpreted what they were seeing, they used their interpretations to create a contrast between what they saw as the joy and contentment of desperately poor Ecuadorans and their own discontent in the midst of material plenty.

The focus on the materialism and commercialism of U.S. culture creates and reinforces an image of the host culture as its polar opposite, as nonmaterialistic, as more authentic and happier. This contrast may result in what we can think of as a "positive" stereotype of the host culture, as something toward which we can aspire. As Chris Weichman, who has been on many other cultural exchanges and mission trips, said to me:

> As a minister, a lot of the work that I do is with people. In a context like the Dominican Republic, you really see that the issues are the same—but they are different. It is easy for Americans to be distracted by a whole lot of—junk. We focus so much on the junk, on the stuff. In other places, there's not as much

junk—I don't quite know how to say what I am getting at. It helps me to see what is extraneous in my life, and what is central. In the Dominican, we see people's relationships with one another. That is what they focus on. A lot of the things that we do are not so relationship based.

In the context of short-term mission, it is important to consider how the stereotypes that participants do create and rely on are often far more favorable toward the "other" culture than their own. We generally think about stereotypes and stereotyping as negative processes, and they certainly can be. However, they are also ways of generalizing about the world, about understanding difference, and about representing cultures, ways that can lead to understanding. Like other forms of travel, short-term mission can encourage or even force participants to question their own cultural biases, their assumptions about what it means to be "poor," and their own culture's perspectives on what is important. This process of questioning is an important, transformative, and maybe even necessary step in gaining cross-cultural perspectives and understanding, as well as in seeing a need to act on those perspectives.

In the contemporary context, scholars and travelers alike find an increased sense of commonality across the globe, through shared religion and global consumerism. Robert Wuthnow, a leading sociologist who studies religion in the United States, notes:

> When Christians from the U.S. go abroad or think about people in other countries, they more easily see these people as being no different from themselves than at any other time in the past . . . [as] fellow Christians who share the same beliefs and practices, though inflected with some cosmetic ethnic differences, just like the person in the adjacent pew at one's own church.[13]

The idea of "global oneness" has positive connotations in American culture.

In conjunction with this sense of a shared humanity, Americans have an awareness of issues of global poverty, evidenced in part through a growing movement in the United States toward voluntarism. A doctor with the Sabaneta team said at dinner one night:

> I don't know if what I do here will change someone's life. You have to tell me that. I am always looking to do that, no matter where I am. In my own life, part of it is learning, for me, that the world is bigger than Erie, Pennsylvania, and there are a lot more people to reach out to. By going out—to Pittsburgh, or anywhere—you intersect with people, you change them, they change you. Because of that change, you return as a different person and do what you were doing differently.

Short-term mission can channel these altruistic impulses in ways that have the potential to help Americans better understand people in geographically distant parts of the world and to truly benefit poor communities and individuals. By encountering other cultures, developing authentic relationships, and learning about people's lives, short-term mission participants gain a greater understanding of the interconnections between cultures.

CROSSING BOUNDARIES

Short-term mission can have a profound impact on travelers' models of the world, allowing them to develop more complex understandings of their own and other cultures. Chris Weichman commented:

> Americans expect people to conform to them, to speak our language. . . . It's like we're the sun and we expect people to rotate around us. It's good to put people in a situation where that isn't likely to happen. Here [in western Pennsylvania], we have an isolated, self-centered, English-speaking culture. We can't separate ourselves from our culture—but we can increase awareness of where we are coming from.

Traveling, being immersed even for a short time in a community with a different language, an unfamiliar currency, an unusual environment, can encourage participants to become more aware of their own cultural assumptions and more open to others. It becomes a physical, material way to reimagine the world and our place in it. Yet to send twenty-five Americans abroad for a week to live in a Dominican neighborhood seems like an expensive way to create the opportunity to learn about culture and stereotyping. Are there other, more persuasive rationales for this kind of exchange?

Short-term mission trips open doors to the possibility of greater cultural understanding. A study of seminary students traveling abroad noted that program goals usually included the idea of developing cultural competencies, including building relationships across differences, broadening student perspectives, and learning about cultural difference. For mission participants, as well as seminary students, it is difficult to actually make concrete gains in these areas during a trip of only a week or two, but progress toward competencies begins in the cross-cultural experience.[14]

Brian Howell, in his thoughtful study of short-term mission in the Dominican Republic, describes the transcendence of culture as an ultimate goal of short-term mission: "Although the narratives of our journey consistently incorporated the expectation of cultural dislocation and unfamiliarity, the triumph of these trips was in seeing how these cultural differences did not matter."[15] The idea that "we are all the same" echoed through the narrative that Howell describes. Cultural transcendence was described as evidenced in a shared Christian identity, found in religious language and ritual,[16] but can also be seen in the way that short-term mission can allow relationships to develop. The emphasis that the Sabaneta team places on the development of relationships is almost impossible to overstate. It was mentioned to me in nearly every interview; it was a frequent topic of discussion at meals; it was brought up by trip leaders at every opportunity during orientations and debriefings. Despite the barriers of language and limited time, team members felt as though they could create bonds of friendship and fellowship with their Dominican counterparts and placed a high value on these relationships. Relationships are what allow participants to transcend stereotypes. As Ralph Hawkins, the New Wilmington pastor, pointed out to the group at dinner one evening, "We have failed if we think of 'The Caribbean,' 'The Dominicans,' or 'The Third World.'" He made prominent air quotes for each of these terms. "There is importance in building relationships, in getting to know people. That is the point of the mission trip. . . . In our work with the Dominicans, it is important to remember that they are not products that we consume, or pictures that we take, but people we know."

Although I sometimes questioned how "relationships" could be developed under the constraints imposed by the structure of the trip, I was impressed by the sincerity of both new and long-term team members in their commitment to creating enduring personal ties. In working with others, serving others, and spending time in a place, the Pennsylvanian travelers come to see "the Dominicans" as individuals with joys and concerns, as families disadvantaged by circumstances, not just as "poor people." It seems to me that this is one of the core benefits of this particular kind of interpersonal exchange. Krista Tippett, a journalist who focuses on religion and interfaith dialogue, said, "Human relationship—which begins with seeing an 'other' as human—is the context in which virtue happens, the context in which character is formed."[17] Relationships are built upon dialogue, listening, opening one's eyes and ears. She suggests that building relationships allows us to create a moral sensitivity that then in turn facilitates creating change in the world. This is another key stated goal of short-term mission, and this is the direction that I will turn to next.

NOTES

1. Marshall Sahlins. "Two or three things that I know about culture." *Journal of the Royal Anthropological Institute* 5, no. 3 (1999): 409.

2. Kevin Birth. "What is your mission here? A Trinidadian perspective on visits from the 'Church of Disneyworld.'" *Missiology* 34, no. 4 (2006): 497–508.

3. Joseph Tortorici, Richard Cunningham, Shenandoah Gale, William Kondrath, and Lisa Withrow. "Cross cultural/intercultural programs in theological schools: A research report from the Wabash Research Team" (Wabash Research Team for Theological School Intercultural Programs, 2011), 22. I am grateful to Dr. Tortorici for sharing the report from this excellent study.

4. Brian Howell. *Short-Term Mission: An Ethnography of Christian Travel Narrative and Experience.* Downers Grove, IL: IVP Academic, 2012, 140.

5. Tortorici et al., 5.

6. Terry Linhart. "Planting seeds: The curricular hope of short term mission experiences in youth ministry." *Christian Education Journal* 2 (Fall 2005): 262.

7. Nelson Graburn. "Secular ritual: A general theory of tourism." In *Hosts and Guests Revisited: Tourism Issues of the 21st Century*, edited by Valene L. Smith and Maryann Brent. Elmsford, NY: Cognizant Communication Corp., 2001, 42, italics in original.

8. Ibid., 48.

9. For example, Tortorici et al., as well as Robert J. Priest, Terry Dischinger, Steve Rasmussen, and C. M. Brown, "Researching the short-term mission movement." *Missiology* 34, no. 4 (2006): 431–450.

10. Dean MacCannell. *The Tourist: A New Theory of the Leisure Class*. New York: Schocken, 1976, 41.

11. Sherry M. Walling, Cynthia B. Eriksson, Katherine J. Meese, Antonia Ciovica, Deborah Gordon, and David W. Foy. "Cultural identity and reentry in short-term student missionaries." *Journal of Psychology and Theology* 34, no. 2 (Summer 2006): 153–164.

12. Linhart, 459.

13. Robert Wuthnow. *Boundless Faith: The Global Outreach of American Churches*. Berkeley: University of California Press, 2009, 26–27.

14. Tortorici et al., 9.

15. Howell, 143.

16. Ibid., 157.

17. Krista Tippett. *Speaking of Faith: Why Religion Matters—and How to Talk about It*. New York: Penguin, 2007, 182.

Chapter Three

Poverty and Economic Development

We visited a lady who had nothing other than her faith in Jesus.
—Sabaneta team member

Some questions are nearly impossible to answer. Why poverty exists in the world is one of them. I teach a course for my students that is rather grandly titled "Ending Poverty." As they file into the classroom on the first day, though, I have to confess to them that there is little truth in advertising here. If I had the simple, foolproof, five-step plan to end poverty, none of us would be there. Last spring, nearing the end of the semester, one student asked what was probably in most of our minds: How can we do anything? The problems are so colossal, how do we make a difference? As I wrestled with possible answers, another student offered a metaphor: "It feels so overwhelming. But think of it like a bucket, and each of us is just a drop. Alone, we are nothing; we are tiny. But if each of us is a drop in that bucket, then it will get filled up. That's really the only way anything ever gets done." His comment at the time reminded me why I teach what I do. It also highlights a perspective that can give heart to those engaged in antipoverty work, including the service experience of short-term missions.

ENCOUNTERING POVERTY

Like the students in my class, participants in short-term missions wrestle with trying to understand poverty and their role in changing conditions for the poor. I met with one participant, Ryan, in my office. A university student, he had recently returned from a short-term mission in Brazil that was focused on providing medical care in a poor urban neighborhood. He brought some pictures of his trip and showed them to me while we talked. Several photos were of a garbage dump, which he said was located next to the neighborhood his group worked in. Showing me a picture of a hillside strewn with litter, he commented, "That's where the children play—their playground." He flipped through a couple more pictures until he found one of the clinic that the medical providers worked in. He showed me another picture that depicted a line of children waiting to be seen. I asked if the medical providers had checked for malnutrition. "Well, we didn't really ask about nutrition," he responded. I then asked whether the trip had been what he expected. He paused, and then replied:

> It's funny, the first day we were at that clinic, it was pretty nice, and I was very surprised. I thought we'd be in tin huts, and traveling just on dirt roads. I thought we'd be staying in a hut. That was what I was prepared for. . . . I was surprised that the poor were right in town. I thought they would be in little villages, more isolated. I thought they'd be out in huts, in their own little tribes. I didn't expect that the poor would be right in the local community. Some of the people we treated in the clinics we would see around town, doing different things.

Working with people who live in poverty is one of the central goals of short-term mission work. Almost by definition, mission groups do not go to work with people in communities or countries wealthier than their own. The groups that host missionaries are defined, then, as being "poor" relative to the missionaries themselves. This encounter with poverty, then, is a central part of the experience and presents a number of challenges to the missionaries themselves, raising questions about what it means to be poor, about the uneven realities of wealth and poverty, about stereotypes and preconceptions about "the poor." Like Ryan, many individuals are conflicted about their encounters with multiple dimensions of poverty—theological, social, political, and experiential.

I have traveled extensively myself, worked with people who did in fact live in small tribes, and seen families who lived in economic misery. As an undergraduate, my choice to study anthropology and my part-time work in a city mental health clinic shaped my ideas of poverty through study and experience. Sometimes I find it difficult to relate to Ryan's image of poverty. For example, I wondered to myself as I read his account where his image that the urban poor could live in "huts" comes from. Why does he think that the poor live in "small tribes" and would never be encountered in their own community running routine errands? His images stand in contrast to my experiences in impoverished communities. I explored this perception further with other mission travelers I interviewed.

Bethany, a university student who traveled to Ghana, explained that when she arrived there: "You saw poverty, all at once. In some senses, it's overwhelming. You come from the wealthy United States, and it's a total shock.

There were one or two days where I cried. It's just so overwhelming—but in a good way." The unfamiliar sights, sounds, and experiences of another culture, and particularly of poverty, create a sense of profound displacement and uncertainty. Some travelers, like Ryan, resort to images from movies and television. Many of the people I interviewed commented on the need to *go*, a need to actually *see for themselves*, and an inability to really *understand* poverty without that direct experience. One student, for example, said: "If people stay here [in the United States], they are very comfortable, they are not interested. [Short-term mission] is something everyone should do. Poverty is a big part of the culture. A lot of people who go there [as tourists] don't see it." Another missionary I interviewed referred to her orientation, explaining: "They told us people were poor, but you don't know [what that means] until you experience it. I didn't *know* people would be *that* poor. They were living in garbage bags over frames."

The mission trip participant might be able—as Bethany was—to frame this as a positive growth experience. I interviewed one student who went on a service trip to Appalachia, who affirmed:

> It was a good experience. People hear about poverty, and they think that it's not that bad, but when you go to poor areas it's very different. It changed my attitude—the people there weren't poor because they made bad decisions; they were born there and would die there. Their kids would stay there. But I see how people get rooted there—it's about family. There is some education, which I guess is aimed at getting some kids a chance to get out. But most people want to stay.

This perspective—that poor people make reasonable choices, based on the same kinds of considerations of family and community on which she might base her own decisions—suggests that this personal encounter with "the poor" can humanize people across geographic and socioeconomic boundaries.

Andrea Lamb, who travels most years to Sabaneta, took her teenage daughter with her one year, in hope, at least in part, that her daughter would gain this broader perspective. Andrea recounted to me:

> We went to one little neighborhood—the only word is squalor. There were animals—it had rained so everything was muddy and yucky. [My daughter] had taken a picture there—and she left it on her dresser for years. I asked her why, why *that* picture, out of all of them, and she said, "So that I remember what it is like to be where people have nothing."

Like Andrea's daughter, travelers may find that their encounter with poverty causes them to reflect on their own cultural values about wealth.

There can be a considerable gap between mission travelers' expectations about the living conditions they are likely to find in the "poor" communities they visit and what they actually encounter. Linda, who traveled to Sabaneta for the first time during the first year of my research, said: "I really thought we were going to be in a concentration camp. I didn't know it would be so developed. I thought the church would be a shack. Not that they would have Facebook and cell phones. We had no idea." She explained that she had lived in Texas, near the border town of Juarez, and had expected to see circumstances that were comparable to or even worse than that, in the Dominican Republic. When I asked if she saw signs of poverty in Sabaneta, another team member suggested that she pictured poverty "like what we would see in Haiti," and that Sabaneta was not "poor like that." Another team member also suggested that people in Sabaneta were not very poor, saying: "This isn't a sleeping in a hammock, eating beans and tortillas experience. You won't find that kind of penetration into poverty, not there [in Sabaneta]." Like Linda, he had spent time in more rural, less well-off regions, and so his perception of poverty in Sabaneta was that it was not severe.

Other team members, unlike Linda, found the poverty more severe than they had expected. One person, for example, described an encounter this way:

> I saw the inside of his house. From the outside, it was like the others, it looks bad. But inside—it was small, with just one room, tin walls, you know, like the roof material, a dirt floor. I don't even know where they store cooked food. There was some formula [for his baby], on the table, because [a team member] had been working on that, but nothing else. It's hitting me now, that there is so much to be done. I don't even know where to start doing it.

Poverty can be hard for mission travelers to understand. The juxtaposition of visible signs of poverty with things that Americans often interpret as signs of wealth or prosperity can be another issue for many travelers. Some people may expect, like Ryan did, that people who are "poor" must lack everything and certainly must not be able to access things that we ourselves may see as "luxuries." A woman who had traveled to Mexico described this sense of incongruity:

> When we arrived at the Indian village, we were shocked to see how dirt poor the people were. There was no electricity, running water, or indoor bathrooms. Even though these people were clearly poor, they showed up to greet the missionaries in their best clothing, which was all designer and probably more expensive than anything we owned. It was clear to us just how proud these people are.

In this case, she did not question where the clothing had come from (possibly from prior mission visits, as clothing donations are a very typical part of many trips), or what it might represent, but simply attributed it to a sense of pride. In another example, when I was in Sabaneta, one of the teenagers was invited to the house of a Dominican boy whom he had befriended. When he returned after his visit, he said that although the two boys did not share a common language, they had connected by playing video games on a console. The adults in the group were a little bemused. "It's just what they would do at home," said his mother.

In describing their perceptions of poverty, whether they felt poverty was severe or not, team members in Sabaneta did not draw distinctions within the Dominican community or recognize the degree to which there was social and economic differentiation. Yet the class divisions within Sabaneta were fairly obvious to me. One day when we were there, I accompanied one of the doctors who was visiting several community members who were unable to travel to one of the clinics because of age or disability. The first was an elderly woman who came out of her small house to greet us, supporting herself carefully with a handmade walking stick. She led us into the house she shared with a grandson. It had a dirt floor and was decorated with carefully hung pages from old calendars intermixed with family photos. From there, we continued up the dirt lane to see a couple who both had multiple serious ailments. They offered us seats on a small sofa in a tiny front room as the doctor set up her travel case on a little table covered with a plastic tablecloth. When she asked about medications, the husband pushed aside the curtain that screened off their bed and came back with an empty bubble packet of pills so worn that I could barely read the label. As the doctor continued her exam, family members and neighbors gathered in the small room, watching and waiting, hoping to have the chance to speak to the American doctor. Ten or twelve consultations later, we worked our way out of the room and proceeded to the last house that we were scheduled to visit in the neighborhood. Standing at the end of the dirt lane, it was a larger house, stuccoed and painted, with a large carved wooden door. A pleasant elderly woman let us in and sat with us on two large stuffed sofas. The floor was gleaming tile, the adjacent kitchen modern and bright. The lady who let us in, the patient, had recently had surgery for breast cancer, which had entailed a trip to a major hospital in the capital. She was doing well in her recovery. Like many other members of the IED congregation in Sabaneta, she could aptly be described as middle class, and she, along with others in the congregation, actively worked to reach out to the larger, less materially fortunate community around her.

Later, I talked to Ralph Hawkins about the team's perceptions of poverty a little more. I told him that I thought that team members had a complex view of the socioeconomic conditions in Sabaneta. Although team members often did refer to their Dominican partners as "having nothing," they were also aware that for many people in Sabaneta, poverty is really not extreme. I mentioned that this may be part of the reason many of the team members are so interested in the Haitian community, since the poverty is more visible there. Ralph mused: "I have never heard anyone say that people aren't poor enough and raise the question of why we are helping them. At least, no one has said that to me." Two explanations of the team's openness to working not just with the very poor, but with a broad range of people occur to me. One is that even the more well-to-do members of the Sabaneta community that the team has met are not "wealthy" by American standards, and so their wealth in contrast to their neighbors goes almost unnoticed. Another possible perspective is that the team members arrive ready to serve all comers, and—just as any of us may need various kinds of assistance at different points in our lives—do not feel the need to draw distinctions between "the poor" who are worthy of help and others who may not "genuinely" need assistance.

How individuals understand and describe "poverty" while on a mission trip can depend on a number of different things, none of which is an objective assessment of actual economic or social conditions "on the ground." One is expectations developed before the trip, which can be shaped not just by formal orientation activities, but also by media images of poverty and stereotypes. Another important factor is the individual's own experiences in poor communities, either in the United States or abroad. Where one person sees utter deprivation, another person can point to signs of some measure of material security, if not wealth. The actual socioeconomic causes of poverty generally remain obscure to the travelers and are not the object of much of their attention.

WEALTH AND POVERTY

What, then, does it *mean* to be poor? There is no single answer to this question, not from an economic perspective, not from a social perspective, and not from an emotional perspective. Poverty is an intrinsic part of the global system, but we also face it on a local level. As I talked to participants in mission trips, I asked about the meanings of poverty. Asking about poverty also led to discussions of wealth and how the short-term mission experience transformed their perceptions of wealth and poverty. Many, if not all, of the people I spoke to were conflicted about the poverty they encountered, but several themes emerged over and over again.

Materialism

Robin is a teacher from central Pennsylvania who has been traveling to Sabaneta for seven years. Because of her vocation and many talents, she usually works with the church youth group in Sabaneta, conducting a variety of musical and educational programs. She confers with the Sabaneta church leaders and tries to gear her programming to issues they suggest for the teens. Last year, one day's lesson focused on materialism and the lure of consumerism. At the end of the day, during a "debrief" of our activities, another team member, a first-timer, quietly commented to me, "It is ironic, Americans talking to Dominicans about materialism." The irony, here, was that American culture is not just more wealthy, but also can be seen as much more materialistic and focused on consumerism. In some ways, of course, the lesson for the Dominican teens was the same as it might be for a similar group sitting in western Pennsylvania—that the value of material goods is not always what it seems and that one needs to be wary of the promises of marketing. And Robin was cognizant that many of the teens in the program came from working- and middle-class families for whom this probably was at least some small concern. But for most mission travelers, one of the most powerful observations they make is that their hosts have a fundamentally different *attitude* toward wealth and possessions.

In some cases, returned travelers were critical of what they saw as typical attitudes of consumerism and materialism in the United States. I was sometimes struck by how common this theme was. Matt, a forty-something traveler to Guatemala, said, "It really made me step back and look at how our own culture is shaped by capitalism and materialism, and question whether that is a good thing." Brittany, a college student, echoed: "Since I have been back in the U.S., I have been a lot more thankful for the things I have. I no longer feel the need to have the best and newest things, and I try to stop complaining about small things." Another student framed her experience more negatively, saying: "The trip changed my view of world, and of America—I don't like living here anymore. The Chinese don't care about materialism, or status, like people here do." Sara, who traveled with her teenaged daughter, claimed that they both learned:

> Stuff doesn't make someone happy. In fact, it makes people miserable. Material objects create unhappiness in many ways. For starters, people have to work more to afford the things that they want. Secondly, the more stuff that's in a person's house, the more they have to clean around. And the material objects themselves take up a lot of a person's time. If someone has a phone or a television, they are going to use them.

Some travelers see gaining a perspective on materialism as a fundamental change in their outlook. Lois, an older woman who travels to Sabaneta, told me:

> At my age, I feel that I've been growing. It has deepened my faith. My worries have turned to concerns. I am ready for what life has to give. Material things

are not so important to me. And I spent over thirty years working in Mary Kay—which is all about the pink Cadillac. It is very materialistic. But I don't let them pressure me anymore. Money is nice, but it is not everything.

Jessica, a traveler to Brazil, said:

> I was impressed by the kid's attitudes. We saw them every day and they could be in the same clothes all ten days. Their lifestyle was poor but it didn't affect their attitude. It makes you think that it is a shame how in the U.S. we are so materialistic. So much money is wasted when people in Brazil can't even shower. I think the trip made a drastic change in my life. I am much less materialistic.

The impact of this realization may be short lived for some, though. One returned missionary recounted that as the memory of the trip fades and everyday life takes over, she has become disappointed in herself. She is starting to fall back into her old lifestyle, finding that material objects are becoming more important to her, and she has to remind herself to be thankful every day.

This attitude of thankfulness is what many travelers see as a key difference between their home culture and the one that they visit. One told me:

> It's so hard to justify how we live in America. We are so wasteful and have so much stuff that we don't need. Even with all our possessions, we are never happy or content. The people down there have nothing, but are always so happy and thankful for what they do have.

Another reflected the same sentiment:

> Americans complain so much about their lives. In general, they get upset and frustrated when the smallest thing goes wrong. In Nicaragua, it was completely different. The people in Nicaragua basically had nothing and yet were filled with such joy. They were thankful for even the smallest things. It was actually really humbling to see.

Being Happy

Another theme, linked to gratitude, is the idea that "the poor" encountered on mission trips are happy in ways that "Americans" aren't. Mission travelers sometimes portray their hosts, unburdened by materialism and the pressure of consumerism, as existentially happier than they are themselves. As one participant commented to me: "I really took notice of how happy people were down there. They were some of the poorest people I had ever seen, and yet they were completely happy."

In some cases where I encountered this attitude, I wondered if the American participants were simply misinterpreting, or perhaps overinterpreting, what were simple norms of politeness in the culture they encountered. One Sabaneta participant, for example, told me, "I just really enjoy going, because people seem happy all of the time." Returned participants frequently describe the culture that they visited as "welcoming," "warm," and "incredibly friendly." One said: "People were always waving to you. They were so happy to see you." My thought is that in a small town, particularly one that receives few tourists, a large group of visibly different strangers is bound to attract some attention.

A more significant theme relating to this idea of happiness contrasts this perception of people as "poor but happy" with American culture and its apparent obsession with material wealth. In this view, materialism, the obsession with status and prosperity, and consumerism are seen as impeding Americans' own ability to be happy. A pastor who traveled to China said:

> This trip really changed my outlook on everyday life. For the first time, I really got to see that material objects don't bring happiness. Americans, as a whole, are very blessed in what they have, and yet they are never happy. They are always concerned with things like cell phones, having the nicest clothes and other material objects. This materialistic obsession really blinds them to what really matters in life. The people there were so much more in touch with what it really means to be alive.

The host communities are seen as more focused on basic needs. The contrast with the expectations of the American travelers was noted by one woman I spoke to, who said: "It's funny because our prayers are always about having more. But they pray for clean water, and food, and just to make it through. It's amazing that they can be happy, and thankful." Another commented: "They are just thankful to wake up in the morning, I guess. We don't have to pray for groceries or for clean water." But travelers to poor communities also draw a deeper contrast, believing that without the distractions of consumerism, the poor are able to focus on more intrinsically satisfying activities and values. One participant said:

> The most important lesson I learned, from both trips I went on, was that our materialism takes away from the time we could be spending with our family or devoting to God. Americans and people from other developed countries feel the need to better people's lives in third world countries, but they may actually be better off than we are because they can see what really matters in life.

The perceptions that people are poor and also welcoming, happy, and generous blend together in the experience of mission travelers. A middle-aged man from Erie said:

My first impression of the local people was just how happy they are. Most of the people the team worked with had nothing, and yet they were always smiling. They were also very generous. Every day the villagers would try to give up their food for the team. They were also always trying to give their pets and handmade crafts to the team members as well. This was really humbling to see. Americans love their possessions and have a hard time letting them go, and that wasn't the case there.

This is another theme that I frequently encountered—that even though poor, the host communities were generous, freely offering what little they had to their visitors. Once again, missionary travelers may underestimate the importance of generosity in many host cultures. But they also contrast those hosts—generous despite their poverty—with people in mainstream American culture, whom they see as selfish and self-centered despite great material abundance.

Peggy McAnlis, one of the medical providers from New Wilmington, said: "People in our group come and see that the people here [in Sabaneta] are not unhappy. They have different priorities. In the U.S., people have much more, materially, but so many are not happy." Another team member added thoughtfully: "Because they *don't* have all the bells and whistles that we have, their faith and relationships are what they have as hobbies. . . . It makes you realize that third world countries aren't as poor as you think they are. They are wealthy in ways that we don't know." American travelers see a contrast in priorities: that the people they visit put more emphasis on family than careers and they spend more time talking to neighbors than shopping. In this set of contrasts, we learn much less about the culture being visited than we do about the traveling Americans themselves. Mission travelers have a tendency to project nostalgic or idealized cultural values on the culture being visited and to find in it the things that the travelers find most lacking in their own culture.

Something else that might contribute to the perception of people in the host culture as happy are the expectations of the Americans themselves that people who are poor must be miserable. Material prosperity is not only an economic condition of American life, but is highly valued and seen as a path to a comfortable and happy life. Even as the mission travelers deplore American materialism, the ideas of upward mobility and economic prosperity are so intrinsically rooted in their own cultural values that many travelers are surprised to find that "the poor" may be reasonably happy on a day-to-day basis. One of the students I interviewed, Brittany, described a little girl she had encountered who, she felt, had become very attached to her during her mission trip:

This little girl came from a really poor family, and the only thing she had to wear was a pair of long-sleeved footsie pajamas. It was terribly hot the entire week, and this girl was always covered with sweat, and yet she was the sweetest, happiest kid I had ever seen. This made me feel terrible every time I even thought about complaining during the trip.

As Brittany encountered what she considered rigorous conditions—little hot water, unreliable electricity, and unusual food—she couldn't imagine how she herself could be happy under those conditions and projected her own expectations onto the host community. As Terry Linhardt, in his study of student short-term missions to Ecuador, also observed:

> They found an appearance of joy and contentment that confronted their own discontentment and consumeristic orientations. The appearances of joy and the realities of poverty were two realities students found paradoxical. As the students tried to understand what they were seeing, they expected to see people languishing and ill-kept, yet they found people who appeared to be content, joyful and loving. [1]

Those of us raised amid the comforts of middle-class American culture can have difficulty separating the ideas of wealth and happiness. Being materially comfortable, we imagine, will (or at least can) foster emotional well-being, while economic destitution must lead to emotional misery. We may have difficulty thinking about other ways of conceptualizing affluence and prosperity. Short-term mission throws the relation between wealth and well-being into stark perspective, offering a different framework, one that anthropologists, beginning with Marshall Sahlins, have noted since the 1960s. [2] Sahlins suggested that poverty is the gap between what someone needs and wants and what is available to them. Prosperity can take one of two forms—producing a lot, or desiring little. Our culture has taken the approach that resources are scarce and that through increasing productivity, we can narrow the gap between what we have and what we need. Even when we have what we need, however, we have found that we *want* more and are never quite satisfied. But another approach, which Sahlins termed the "Zen road to affluence," suggests that resources are plentiful, and material wants are few and limited and can be easily met. In this way, people can find it possible to achieve affluence—defined as having enough—by desiring little. In this view, we have a lot to learn from less industrialized cultures.

Sahlins's framework can be helpful in certain ways, but it is limited in others. It does help in understanding how we conceptualize poverty and what it means. It may explain why some individuals in communities that host mission groups do not live in a state of angst over what the travelers may see as poor conditions and why they instead focus on dimensions of life other than the material. Where it is less helpful, however, is in conceptualizing the nature of global poverty in the twenty-first century, with a global economy oriented toward consumer capitalism. This framework does not help us distinguish between wants and needs or to understand what level of consumption is adequate. And it could let us justify poverty and deprivation with the excuse that some people do not want more than what they have and that somehow our culture is entitled to a higher level of consumption than others. It does throw some light on our own ethnocentric assumptions, however, and perhaps leads us to question the level not of others' desires but our own. Many returned missionary travelers come to see their own level of consumption through new eyes. They recognize that we invest a great deal of time and energy in a quest for an ever-increasing array of consumer goods, sacrificing many things in order to bridge the gap between wants and needs. Some mission travelers come to see the American ethic of consumption and materialism as a burden rather than as a goal, a tragedy of our modern lifestyle rather than a model to hold up for others.

Material Poverty, Spiritual Wealth

Another key theme that emerges in many mission trip participants' thinking about poverty is found in their understanding of the relationship between poverty and spirituality. They strongly link what they perceive to be a simple life to a greater sense of religious devotion and see material poverty as equivalent to, or a sign of, spiritual wealth, a deep theme in Christianity and especially in Protestantism. "Has not God chosen those who are poor in the eyes of the world to be rich in faith and to inherit the kingdom he promised those who love him?"[3]

Many travelers made this association. A pastor from Erie said: "Even though these people were extremely poor, they were also happy and spiritual. They were more enthusiastic about God and church than most of the people who attend churches back home." Again, travelers often make a comparison between the host community and the home community. Julie, a young Spanish teacher who chose her career based on a trip as a high school student to Sabaneta, said: "The people have nothing, but it doesn't matter. They are so aware and present and thankful in the life of the church. In the U.S., we have so many distractions."

In numerous interviews, I heard comments suggesting that an association between poverty and spirituality is not just coincidental, but that it can be seen as causative: that being poor enables a greater relationship with God. One participant said: "I think that God shows me other types of people, and he helps me to know them. The landscape there is very beautiful. The people there are so much stronger. People have nothing and they are closer to God. They are very humble. It encourages me to get closer to God." This woman believed the experience of poverty made people that she encountered strong in ways that she felt were not routinely possible for those living a less deprived North American lifestyle. Another participant made this point even more clearly: "I almost feel that people in less developed countries are more blessed than we Americans are. They worry about things like feeding their kids and having a place to sleep. These are such real concerns that they have no other choice but to put their faith in God." Here, the desperation of poverty—how to feed your children, the fear of not having a secure home—is seen as a condition that creates greater faith.

Of course, mission teams encounter people who are not poor and people who are not religious. But the strong symbolic associations between spiritual wealth and material poverty seem to withstand what could be seen as discrepancies. They view those who are poor and religious, as we have seen, as being close to God, with a deep faith that sustains them. Examples of this stand out most clearly to the mission travelers. In contrast, when Americans encounter people who are poor but not religious, they argue that these people would be better off, both materially and spiritually, if they did have a religious commitment. Sometimes they observe that a relationship with God is hampered by extreme poverty. "If there is someone in dire poverty, they are not going to be able to listen [to a religious message]," one Sabaneta traveler commented. To reach the extremely poor, in this view, the first step is to begin to meet those material needs and to demonstrate love in doing so. People who are materially comfortable and religiously devout are in a sense the success stories of faith, of what one can accomplish with hard work and a good relationship with God. And finally, those who are materially wealthy but lack religious devotion prove the point that the poor are closer to God, free of the temptations and vices that wealth can bring.

The views that mission participants hold about poverty are complex, but poverty is usually seen as morally uplifting. Mission trip participants generally frame the pitfalls of their own culture's relative prosperity in terms of the dangers of decadence: a lack of gratitude, taking things for granted, the pressure on families and individuals to be successful and the constraints that this can put on our time and energies. The host culture is imagined as embodying the opposite of these pressures, a kind of counter-example. In a kind of nostalgia for the present, mission travelers admire the host culture for avoiding the problems of modernity they see in their own culture.

For many mission participants, the trip itself offers them an opportunity to serve the poor, to step outside the values they see in their own culture. As travelers like Brittany encounter material poverty, it makes them more aware of their own comfortable world. Some participants feel challenged, because the differences raise uncomfortable questions about the conditions in the global economy that create such profoundly different circumstances for different individuals. The trip could also foster a sense of guilt. How can I complain about my circumstances, after all, when so many people are worse off? But service offers the opportunity to redeem this uneasiness to transcend both economic and geographic distance and to "make up for" the travelers' relatively fortunate circumstances. The poverty of the community that the group travels to is the context in which this transformation happens.

The irony here, of course, is that mission participants see the poverty of the host culture as a genuine problem. The specters of hunger, shoddy housing, inadequate education, and other impediments to a quality life are a great concern to mission travelers, and indeed, mission trips are often designed around service projects intended specifically to alleviate these problems, at least in some small way. The idealization of poverty as a spiritual blessing, then, means that ending, or transforming, poverty can seem ambivalent, holding out the possibility that the host culture could fall into the same pitfalls of materialism and shallowness as North America has.

One of the benefits of short-term mission, and perhaps one of the reasons it has become so popular in the United States, is that it does encourage its American participants to question their assumptions about wealth and poverty. Mark Radecke, who has done research on short-term mission, finds that when participants "meet hardworking, intelligent, honest, and caring people who are poor beyond their imagination, they have to conclude that the poverty of their new acquaintances is the result of more than a series of bad choices and a string of bad luck,"[4] and they start to gain a greater understanding of the role of structural factors in creating conditions of poverty. "They grapple with the reality of sin so expertly woven into the fabric of social structures that its presence becomes virtually undetectable to the untrained eye."[5] Becoming aware of the nature of poverty and inequality is the first step in making meaningful change.

THE BUCKET: GLOBAL POVERTY

Short-term missions are a way for participants to develop just such an awareness of the nature of poverty. In Sabaneta, I walk with Richard Taylor from the team's base at the secondary school in Sabaneta over to "The Barrio," a mostly Haitian enclave. As we cross a busy road, we move from the middle-class neighborhood where the school is located to a more economically diverse one. Neat stucco houses, painted cheerfully in pinks and greens, alternate with structures of unpainted cement block. As we continue, the road grows narrower, and we turn down a dirt lane. Here, the cement block houses take on an air of permanence and solidity, compared with the neighboring houses, which are little more than makeshift shanties with walls of scavenged corrugated tin and mismatched boards. I spot a rat scurrying under one of the walls. Richard, who hails from Tennessee, is a well-known figure in the Barrio, and as we walk, we are joined by a few children. He stops frequently to exchange a few words in Creole or Spanish with men and women who stand in open doorways or sit in plastic chairs or on upturned buckets in front of their tiny houses. Richard, who founded a small aid organization that provides various kinds of support to Barrio residents, quietly informs me as we walk that a particular small shack, on our right, is home to about fourteen people, and that this man on our left lost his wife last year to AIDS. Richard frequently guides strangers, usually foreign short-term missionaries, on tours through the Barrio, so my presence causes little stir. Children, mostly barefoot, follow along behind us as we continue on our way.

The question of why people are poor is hardly a new one. One underlying consideration has to do with human nature. Here, answers tend to swirl around two persistent poles. One is based on the assumption that the individual is a rational being, understanding and acting in his or her self-interest. This approach suggests that rational individuals are poor only because they face particular deficits—education, capital, or freedom. If these deficits are remedied, the individual will, almost inevitably, be able to emerge from poverty, because he or she will make choices that allow him or her to do so. In this view, poverty is an *individual* condition, and so the remedy to poverty must also be, essentially, at the level of the individual.

A second approach suggests that an individual is shaped by life circumstances—that social context takes precedence over innate behavior. Poverty, then, is a result of social conditions that are largely outside the control of any individual. Instead, the circumstances of the individual are shaped by history, society, traditions, and social structures that can only be changed through collective action, government intervention, transformation through time, or other large-scale forces. In this view, poverty is a *social* condition, and poverty must be dealt with at the level of social groups.

Reality may fall in between these two positions. Individuals are shaped by social forces, but they also have agency to make choices and change the circumstances they are in. Poverty is a result of the relation between markets and the obscure movements of capital, on the one hand, and the ways in which ordinary people make a living, on the other hand. Individuals are rational economic actors, but they are also motivated by a host of noneconomic concerns, and their economic relations are embedded within social relationships. People who are poor behave in ways that make sense from their own point of view, and they are also limited by their circumstances. The causes of poverty exist at both a social level and an individual level.

What does this understanding mean in terms of real people? In walking through the Haitian Barrio, where children ran in ragged clothing and houses were patched with scavenged packing crates, we passed a number of people chatting on cell phones. One of the team members mentioned this to me, not unkindly, but as an example of choices that he did not understand. "I don't know how much they cost, but it must be something—money that folks could spend on more important things." According to the view that poverty is a result of individual choices, a cell phone would be an example of bad choices—frivolously spending money that could be used to support a family in more productive ways. The second view might lead us to conclude that a cell phone user was duped into thinking that a cell phone increased his or her social status and felt socially pressured to have one. Taking a third perspective, however, would encourage us to probe a little deeper and consider other possibilities. Perhaps the guy on the phone had gotten a call from a possible employer who is more likely to hire day laborers he can reach easily, or maybe he was talking to relatives across the international border with Haiti. I honestly don't know how much a cell phone costs in the Dominican Republic; however, cell phones and cell service are generally much less expensive in developing countries than they are in the United States, and cell phones are less expensive and more readily available than traditional land lines. As elsewhere in the developing world, many people use prepaid phones or pay by usage rather than on a monthly plan, making them much less expensive than the smartphone in my pocket, even when we calculate that cost not in dollars paid but as a percentage of a monthly budget. Our cell phone user is likely more cognizant of the realities of his budget than we are and has made a decision that a phone is worth the expense, given his other needs and the benefits of having the phone. Rather than deplore his choice as irrational or misguided, better to try to understand it, to reflect on his priorities and needs rather than ours.

Americans often see poverty as a material problem, as a shortage or lack of resources. This view makes a great deal of sense on an intuitive level: If people are poor, then by definition they face material want. We could make a list—they lack food, water, housing, or health care. This understanding could be extended further, to define poverty based on a standard of living within a community or region and to define a poor person as one who lacks resources relative to that standard. The notion of poverty as relative is helpful, in that it allows us to see that poverty can exist in communities that are wealthier than others, and that a standard of living that would make a person "poor" in one region, such as the United States, would outstrip the very "wealthiest" person in a remote village somewhere. But this view still focuses on having, or lacking, resources themselves. Thus understood, poverty must be a shortage or scarcity of resources, either globally or locally. And the solution to poverty, if not exactly simple, is a relatively straightforward process of creating more resources and moving them around.

On closer examination, however, poverty is more complex, and more insidious, than a simple lack of resources. Certainly, from the perspective of fourteen people living in an inadequate, makeshift shelter, we can understand poverty as such. But on a larger social level, poverty is about power and access to resources. The problem, except in specific instances where large-scale natural disasters or warfare have occurred, is not that resources are scarce or unavailable, but that resources are not evenly distributed and that some people within a society do not have the ability to access the resources they need—whether through employment, public welfare programs, family networks, or some other means. Seen in this way, then, poverty is inherently a political problem.

For the fourteen people living in a tin shack, addressing poverty from this political perspective leads us to some larger questions. It leads us not just to ask how to get a larger house built, but also to question the status of Haitian workers and families within the Dominican Republic. Many are illegal, and although it is possible for illegal workers to gain employment there, both working conditions and rates of pay are poor. It would lead us to consider longer-term historical circumstances that have led so many impoverished Haitians to try their luck in the Dominican Republic, despite the physical and social challenges involved. And it may lead us to more persistent questions of race and discrimination, not just in the Dominican Republic, but also in the Caribbean and across the hemisphere. Viewing poverty from a political perspective raises larger questions about power and resources, the history of colonialism, the current role of the United States and other global powers in developing countries, and the global economic system in the twenty-first century.

From this perspective, we come to understand that tackling poverty is not merely a technical challenge. Building a house only adds a drop of water to a bucket overflowing with significant historical and social issues. To make a significant difference in conditions of poverty, we have to examine these underlying conditions. Poverty is not accidental, but rather an outcome of a system of power. Only by demanding changes in that system will we be able to bring resources to people who lack them. Changing conditions of poverty, by making fundamental changes to how resources are distributed, is really changing systems of power, not just stuff. But the problem is solvable.

The way we conceptualize poverty is important because the solutions—or at least steps toward solutions—we propose depend on our understanding of the cause. And, as I will discuss later, while much antipoverty work happens at the level of "drops of water," one individual and family at a time, when we understand poverty on a societal scale, when we keep a larger perspective in mind, we can develop more effective interventions.

POVERTY AND GLOBALIZATION

When we look at poverty from a larger perspective, both historical circumstances and the patterns of the contemporary global economy shape local economic systems. Every population in the world is affected by globalization. Even in remote regions, we find mass-produced consumer goods, international media outlets, and economic opportunities shaped by forces that are not local, but rather regional, national, and transnational. It has become commonplace to talk about globalization as a phenomenon that affects us all, but it isn't always clear what "globalization" means and how it affects individuals. What is "global," and what is "local"?

In some ways, globalization is not a new phenomenon. In the eighteenth and nineteenth centuries, millions of migrants moved from Europe to the Americas, for example. Going back further, we can trace the movements of people and commodities during the colonial era, which radically reshaped "local" systems both in colonized regions and in the imperial centers. We can go further back, to times when the great empires of the preindustrial world linked far-flung regions to obtain goods both precious and utilitarian. And back even further, archaeologists can trace the movement of goods and populations during the Stone Age over trade routes that are truly astounding.

Yet even if we have always been truly interconnected, over the past century those linkages have grown more intense, more immediate, and more encompassing than they were in the past. When my great-grandparents migrated from Europe to New England, they made a one-way journey that took a month or more, with no expectation of returning even for a visit. The only news they received from home came in the form of occasional letters. Today's migrants from the Dominican Republic to the United States, in contrast, have every expectation of being able to move back and forth easily, at least for visits and vacations, and can be instantaneously in contact with family members through phones and social media. On a larger scale, capital and financial markets are thoroughly and immediately interconnected, so that small economic forces in one region can have a ripple effect through the global economy.

Globalization has both economic and cultural dimensions, and although these are linked to each other in myriad ways, separating these dimensions may help us to think about them. Culturally, styles and trends spread rapidly, with elements from different regions combining and recombining in ways that are often creative and innovative. In the early 1990s, predictions were that cultural globalization would lead to a kind of homogenization of the world, as people became consumers of a common media and followed the same trends. As time has gone on, reality has proven to be much more complex. Local languages continue to be lost at a rapid pace, for example, even as ethnic identity has continued to play a central role in political movements and local culture. Folk traditions—clothing, handicrafts, music—have found new audiences, even as inexpensive mass-produced clothing and tools have put many local artisans out of business. People and governments show an increased recognition of the value of ethnic diversity, pluralism, and human rights, even as many regions suffer from ethnic and other identity-based tensions.

On an economic level, globalization has reshaped the world. Global capitalism affects us as workers and producers and as consumers—no less in the small communities of western Pennsylvania than in the Barrios of Sabaneta or anywhere else. And it also affects us in complex ways, sometimes beneficial and sometimes detrimental. Those affects are not random, but are an integral part of the system of global capitalism, in which opportunities are not evenly distributed. The logic of the global economy is to increase production and to increase profits and capital that go to business owners and shareholders.

Whether I am in Puerto Plata or Pittsburgh, I could decide to buy a pair of jeans. In either case, the jeans I look at are probably imported from somewhere else. Like most people, I don't want to spend more money on them than I have to, and I look around for an inexpensive option. The cost of my jeans depends on the price of the material and on the costs of putting them together. The cost of the materials is based on a global market, so manufacturers are unlikely to be able to control that very much. Companies can increase their profit by making the jeans somewhere where labor is less expensive and regulations are minimal, lowering their costs and passing that savings on to me. Although this manufacturing practice may extend employment into impoverished regions throughout the world, the conditions of that employment may be harsh. The benefits of this system do extend to both me and my neighbor in Sabaneta as consumers of inexpensive products. But as a first-world consumer, I don't pay as much of a price in terms of my employment options, my working conditions, or the conditions of my community as do the workers and consumers in poorer regions. In many parts of the world, the global economy can make people poorer, because the benefits—in the form of profits from manufacturing, financial transactions, agriculture, and other enterprises—go mostly to a very small part of the population, to owners and shareholders, who may ultimately be in other, wealthier countries, while poor countries "race to the bottom" in terms of wages and working conditions.

In the Haitian Barrio, team members were often surprised to learn how little people earned—often less than US$10 a day, for irregular work with no benefits or security.[6] Even people in the country legally earned little more. Although $10 is "worth more" there, in terms of purchasing power, than in the United States, it is still not an adequate income. People work for less than a living wage for many reasons, however. Even a low wage is preferable to no income at all, and families often try to manage by pooling the incomes of several workers. Low-wage workers compete for jobs, and individuals may accept a low wage because they have no bargaining power with employers, who can always find someone else.

Haitian residents in the Barrio may face additional obstacles in finding work. One Haitian man, Jean, recounted to one of the team doctors that he would like to work in the Dominican Republic and has a visa that gives him legal status, but he cannot find a job, partly because jobs are scarce and partly because of deeply rooted racism. Like others we spoke to, he works irregularly doing construction. His wife, like many other Haitians, works as an itinerant vendor, buying clothes in Haiti and selling them from a cart that she wheels through the streets of Sabaneta. This kind of work—people being in business for themselves selling fruit, clothing, small household items—is common. This kind of work places these folks in what is called the "informal economy"—a kinder term for a black market—of entrepreneurs working outside the supervision of the government, lacking permits and licenses, not collecting or paying taxes, not reporting their income on any kind of official level. Around the world, people who work in the informal economy also do not receive benefits that are tied to employment, such as public health care, retirement benefits, or worker protections. The informal economy is a large part of daily life throughout the developing world,[7] however, and includes essential activities like child care, transportation, and food services, which are not intrinsically illegal (as would be selling drugs or engaging in prostitution, for example). The informal economy provides a vital niche for people like Jean and his wife, despite its drawbacks. In the Dominican Republic, nearly half of all workers have jobs in the informal economy.[8]

The connections between the formal and informal sectors of the economy, between Haitian migrant workers and American consumers, between "the poor" and the "wealthy" in different parts of the world, can be challenging to trace. Yet understanding these connections is a critical step in understanding the causes of poverty. Inexpensive consumer goods in the United States make my life easier but are the result of low wages in other parts of the world. People are interconnected—as consumers, as workers, as members of the global economy and global system—in unprecedented ways. The costs and benefits of this dynamic system are uneven.

CONCEPTUALIZING ECONOMIC DEVELOPMENT

Since the 1950s, governments and international agencies have made efforts to alleviate regional poverty through economic development. Anthropologist Arturo Escobar traces the ways in which our current understandings of economic development took shape in the decades after World War II.[9] During the colonial era, global poverty was considered by those in the wealthier parts of the world as an outcome of supposed "backwardness," and to the extent that it was seen as a problem, the responses were paternalistic and ethnocentric. After World War II, as industrialization, commercial agriculture, and global capitalism spread, traditional systems of production were disrupted, sometimes because land and labor were needed for industrial production and sometimes because of policies that encouraged "modernization." Global inequality was perceived by policymakers as a lack of "progress" and "development" in poorer regions, and they saw technology and industrialization as "fixes" for the problems of poverty. Proponents of this postcolonial model believed that if poor nations could just emulate the United States and Western Europe economically, through increased industrialization and modernization, poverty would fade away.

In the ensuing decades, of course, poverty proved to be a much more intractable problem. Strategies of modernization, rather than solving the problem, tended to create rapid urbanization and to concentrate wealth in the hands of a very small upper class. Cold war politics took precedence over humanitarian concerns, as the United States and the Soviet Union offered economic aid as either a carrot or a stick to lure the elite of poor countries toward particular political decisions and to entice them toward strategic alliances. Alternative strategies, such as plans to replace expensive imported goods with less expensive products manufactured locally, or nationalizing key industries, sprang up and then faded, failing to make poverty, or poor people, go away.

Ideas about poverty and development can be broken down into three major schools of thought. First, those who follow a conventional view see development as a series of more or less successful interventions that attempt to make people less poor. For example, development professionals could create a specific program to increase levels of education and measure whether the program succeeded or failed. Successful programs can then be replicated and unsuccessful approaches abandoned. This approach tends to lead to an emphasis on measurable outcomes—houses built, children vaccinated, and so on—rather than less quantifiable factors such as happiness or well-being. But it is useful for identifying concrete, specific strategies and approaches that may alleviate suffering and offer aid to individuals, families, and communities. The emphasis on assessment of results does offer some reassurance, to donors and volunteers, that services have been provided to those in need.

An example from the Haitian Barrio can illustrate this approach. There, the Sabaneta team provided a team of doctors for a day who saw patients, dispensed medications, and recommended tests. The morning of their visit, I sat with Jonathan Miller, one of the American doctors, doing my best to help as a translator. We set up in a pew in the church built by Richard's foundation, with another pew turned around in front of us to provide a seat for the patient. The large sanctuary was filled with those waiting, and children, neatly dressed for the visit, roamed around. There was no privacy; those waiting usually maintained a distance that was more symbolic than functional. Because many of those seeking care spoke limited Spanish, and neither Jon nor I spoke Creole, communication was challenging and sometimes involved a second translator, usually a Haitian neighbor, who could translate from Spanish to Creole and back to Spanish, so I could translate to the doctor in English. The consultation would usually include a summary of the immediate problem and maybe a brief medical history. Jon would sometimes take a blood pressure or a temperature—in part, as several of the doctors had explained to me, because people expected it and liked the hands-on contact. Medications, mostly antibiotics and painkillers, were dispensed from another set of pews in the back of the hall. At the end of the morning, Jon and I stopped in a small house to see an elderly lady who was unable to travel the short distance to the clinic, so we could bring her some measure of palliative care. For the people in the community, for whom even basic health care represents a major expense, this care, provided at a very nominal fee, met some of their immediate needs.

For the Barrio clinic, we could count the number of patients seen and the numbers of pills dispensed. We could categorize and enumerate the ailments that were treated. With a little more systematic data collection than we actually undertook, we could have constructed a public health profile of the neighborhood. Although the medical care provided might have been meager, in comparison to a systematic health care system that would also provide long-term follow-up and more sophisticated tools for diagnosis and treatment, the day clinic met its immediate goals of serving the most pressing needs of the community.

A second view of development can be broadly referred to as political economy. From this perspective, the emphasis is less on whether a program or project was successful and more on whose interests were served. A more critical approach, this focuses on how programs meet the needs of the system, rather than the needs of the individual. For example, a literacy program is viewed as a way to educate a labor force to meet employers' needs for more skilled workers. Although this approach offers less immediate, practical strategies than the former, it does open up a bigger window onto projects and programs. It leads us to question whether or not the recipients of aid really benefit, and if so, how. It encourages us to think about larger systems of power and inequality. Why are people poor in the first place? Who benefits from systematic inequality?

Once again, we can apply this formulation to the clinic in the Barrio. Although not denying that we saw a boy who was clearly in need of an antibiotic for an ear infection, we would find that the mother of that boy was in the Dominican Republic illegally and so did not feel safe bringing her child to the public clinic in a nearby neighborhood. Her illegal status was not uncommon in the community; many of the Haitians have inadequate paperwork and work permits. They migrate in order to escape more intolerable conditions in their home country and to earn the higher wages that can be found a short distance across the border. They are hired illegally, because they work for less than legal laborers and are not entitled to any health or safety protections. Even the Haitians who are in the country legally face discrimination and low wages. Low wages, mostly in the agricultural sector, allow commodities like sugar to be produced inexpensively and exported to the global market. Wealthy landowners and business owners benefit, as do international (including American) consumers. From this perspective, an antibiotic for an earache is merely a bandage that enables a larger system to continue to function and perhaps even hides or masks some of the intolerable conditions that are created by the system. The solution, then, is not just more or better health care, but a reconfiguration of working conditions that would allow low-wage workers the means to sustain themselves and their families.

A third, and more abstract, approach points us to the language we use to define issues of poverty and their solutions. The term *development* itself has connotations of growth, of increasing capital, of becoming more modern and more materially wealthy. Development is assumed to be universally desirable and politically neutral. The term leaves us with very little question about whether more wealth should be the goal. Being happy, living securely, contributing to others, and maintaining cosmic harmony are not part of the idea of "development." The focus of development is on ensuring more efficient production rather than more fulfilling lives. The argument here is that the words we use to talk about a topic also represent abstract symbols and ideas, and that these layers of meaning become part of the topic in ways that are not always readily apparent. A discourse develops that defines problems in a particular way and then leads us to particular kinds of solutions. This is not negative in and of itself, but discourse can act to "screen out" other kinds of ways of framing both problems and solutions.

Sometimes the metaphor of a game can be helpful in understanding how a discourse works: A discourse provides the rules of the game, which all of the players understand. In a game such as baseball, there are players, there are rules, there is a field, and there is specific equipment. The Red Sox can't win by throwing rocks at the Yankees or by making a field goal. Even the idea that they could try that is faintly ridiculous. The discourse of baseball defines the ideas behind the game, the resources that can be used, the rules of play, who participates and how, the expected behaviors, and the appropriate ways to complain about the results. It shapes the game, and it also shapes how we think about the game. On a larger scale, the discourse of baseball *is* the reality of baseball, because players and spectators agree about what should happen.

Although this analysis of discourse is based on theories that touch on the very nature of reality and power and how they are represented, it can be helpful on a practical level, because it highlights the assumptions that different people and organizations bring to antipoverty work. Within the sphere of international development work, the discourse of development focuses on particular themes and ideas and shapes the ways programs and projects are conceptualized, funded, and implemented. No specific entity, government, or organization controls or "sets" these emphases, but as with any kind of discourse, development discourse shapes the expectations and agendas of those involved in antipoverty work at an international level.

Using this kind of theoretical focus reminds us that development is only one context for understanding social relations and people's lives. To apply this framework to the clinic in the Barrio, I rely on the sensitivity and deep human caring of the American doctor I interpreted for, Jon. Thinking of him as a "doctor," meeting with each of his "patients" throughout the morning, we would certainly not fault him for adhering to a kind of medical "script," focusing on immediate physical complaints and symptoms, perhaps a brief medical history, a diagnosis, and a recommendation. In the context of the clinic, with a long line of people waiting to be seen, this would have seemed perfectly appropriate. But Jon would pause and ask me to find out whom the patient lived with and where his or her house was—not to warn against infection or collate public health data, but to demonstrate his interest and concern for his or her circumstances. He listened thoughtfully as one explained that she had left Haiti so she could send money back to her family there. He stepped outside of his role as doctor and allowed her to step outside of her role as patient, so that he could connect with her in a more personal way. This exchange did not produce any result that could be measured, but it did reframe the encounter in a way that allowed Jon to explore the actual conditions and meaning of "poverty" in a different kind of way. Although this different understanding alone did not and could not enable Jon to meet his patient's immediate, physical, medical needs, it did allow him to take other actions to meet those needs in a way that was more sensitive, and perhaps more humanizing, than would otherwise have been the case.

Understanding the actions of Jon and the other doctors through the lens of development discourse opens us up to a broader understanding of what "development" is and what its goals are. Using the lens of political economy may help us to see the clinic in a context larger than what happened in the room. And a conventional view focuses us on immediate goals and outcomes in providing health care. Separately, none of these three approaches to understanding the value of the mission clinic in the Haitian Barrio gives us the entire picture. Taken together, they can provide complementary perspectives that help us to better understand poverty and programs aimed at alleviating poverty.

POVERTY AND DEVELOPMENT

One perhaps surprising result of understanding economic development from multiple perspectives is that it can sometimes worsen, rather than improve, the lives of people with few material resources. Anthropologists, who have long worked with peoples often referred to as "tribal" or "remote," have suspected that "development" could cause, rather than remedy, poverty. Rather than creating positive benefits, development has sometimes brought economic and cultural assimilation, reduced access to land for traditional subsistence activities, and produced social dislocation. Poor people were not being "left behind" or "left out" of the development process but were being integrated into global capitalism at the lowest level.[10] As industrialization, modernization, and global capitalism have spread, they have incorporated even the most remote populations. Yet we do not have to seek out "remote" or "indigenous" people to see the calamitous effects of global capitalism for some populations. We merely need to walk through the Barrio or through urban shantytowns or the shacks of migrant agricultural workers throughout the world. And although some romantics may suggest that the solution is to "go back" to slower, more traditional ways of living, a more realistic assessment indicates that this is impossible, and for many people in those communities, undesirable. In order to create meaningful change, it is incumbent on those of us with power and resources within the global system to critically examine ways in which those who are disenfranchised in various ways in the current system can have better access not just to wealth but to a lifestyle that promotes human dignity.

A prominent advocate of promoting human dignity is economist Amartya Sen, winner of the 1998 Nobel Prize in Economics. In a world where neither wealth nor opportunities are evenly distributed, Sen defines poverty not as a lack of resources but as a lack of choices.[11] He points out, quite reasonably, that no person chooses deprivation if he or she has alternatives. Sen suggests that rather than trying to increase wealth, then, we focus on increasing choices. When individuals, families, and communities are able to make decisions and maintain their own autonomy, poor people, like the rest of us, can choose what is best, as they see it. Sen encourages us to recognize that what is "best" may be socially and culturally specific. He also suggests a number of ways in which the choices available to individuals can be improved or enhanced. One is through increasing the quality of education and raising literacy, which promote thoughtful citizenship and boost job possibilities. Another is to support gender equality, without which literally half the population has its choices constrained. Low poverty and low unemployment are factors that Sen sees as not just economically beneficial, but as means to expand choices. Fostering ecologically sustainable practices, which use the natural world without destroying natural resources or compromising long-term ecological productivity, is also advocated by Sen. For people in dire circumstances, sustainability may seem like an unaffordable luxury, but without it, their long- and even medium-term choices will be limited. Sen also points to two factors that we usually think of as political rather than economic that improve people's ability to make good choices: political equality and democratic systems of government. With meaningful participation in government and the political process, he argues, people will support structures and policies that will expand opportunities and freedoms. Taken as a whole, Sen's approach shifts the emphasis in thinking about development to the infrastructures that undergird people's lives and create change on the larger scales of nation and region, as well as at the local level. Instead of focusing on strictly economic, measurable outcomes, it points us toward ideas of freedom, autonomy, and empowerment and opens up new ways of framing the discourse of working against poverty.

Anthropologist and physician Paul Farmer takes a somewhat different approach from Sen.[12] He asks simply, if curable illness can be cured, preventable illness can be prevented, and controllable illness can be controlled, why aren't they? He reminds us that poverty and deprivation are not accidents, nor are they random in either their distribution or effects. Social forces, power, and inequality put some people but not others at risk of suffering. In order to alleviate suffering, it is critical to acknowledge and confront underlying issues of inequality. Farmer and others suggest that individuals and organizations use three overlapping approaches to try to solve social issues and problems of poverty. The first is to offer charity, in which a generous and benevolent donor simply allocates goods and services to the poor. An approach based on charity often lacks a systematic strategy for dealing with poverty, responding to needs in only a piecemeal way.[13] Although it may be warranted in cases of emergency and disaster aid, Farmer cautions that this model is paternalistic and ultimately puts the recipients of charity in a position of powerlessness and inferiority. A better, but still problematic, approach is to promote development, in line with the conventional approach I discussed earlier. Development approaches problems caused by poverty in a more strategic way, trying to share the benefits of capitalism or create humanizing reforms within the system. Although development may be effective according to some measures, it can also perpetuate systems of inequality and rests on a basic assumption that the poor are backward. The third approach, advocated by Farmer, is to uphold social justice, transforming the social conditions that create and maintain poverty.

THINKING DIFFERENTLY

Building relationships, providing services, and meeting people's needs are components of the work of short-term mission teams. In Sabaneta, the medical team provides staff and medications at a small public clinic that is directly across the street from the IED church and school. Each morning, patients begin to congregate in the front courtyard at the clinic, receiving a number in the queue from the clinic staff. As the missionary team prepares for the morning's work, the courtyard fills with parents and children first sitting on cement benches around its periphery, then standing just outside the low courtyard wall. In the minutes before the doctors begin to accept their first patients, one of the pastors from the church usually leads the waiting crowd in a short prayer and often a song. Although many of the patients are church congregants, others are not. If there is time, some of the medical providers join the group.

I listened one morning as the pastor offered a prayer of thanks for the visiting team and reminded the patients that "sometimes people think that the Americans come because they are rich and have a lot of money, but it is because they love them that they come." For the American team, the notion that their Dominican counterparts saw them as wealthy created a bit of discomfort. Although the "poverty" of their Dominican hosts occasioned conversation, like most Americans, they tended to see themselves as middle class. For many team members, the trip itself required financial sacrifice, often replacing a vacation or some other luxury. In addition to their own travel expenses, many donated directly to church projects, helped to support Dominican families financially, or provided money to the church school's scholarship program. One team member explained to me that she asked her grown children and their families to contribute to this fund rather than to exchange traditional Christmas gifts. At a meeting of the parents and students who received scholarships, one of the team members explained to the listening group that each scholarship represented a lot money for them, but also a lot of money for their American donors.

How we think about and talk about wealth and poverty is important, especially for the ways in which our assumptions shape our perceptions of the situation of others and the ways in which our assumptions then shape our actions. The way we define problems—in this case, the problem of poverty—leads us to certain kinds of solutions. If our definition is faulty, our solutions will not be effective—or at least, not effective in the way that we intended them to be.

When we turn to the issue of poverty, we can see that the ways we define the problem shape the kinds of solutions we believe might help. This clear understanding then facilitates our examination of conditions of poverty and the results of interventions. In many approaches to changing conditions of poverty, the focus is on economic growth, on capital, on becoming more modern, and on becoming more materially wealthy. Yet from this chapter, we can begin to see that development can be understood in a broader way, one which emphasizes quality of life and the support of individual fulfillment. We can see that goals such as being happy, living securely, and contributing to the well-being of others may be more important than income. When we understand our goals, we can begin to formulate plans and projects that will help us achieve them.

NOTES

1. Terry Linhardt. "They were so alive!: The spectacle self and youth group short-term mission trips." *Missiology* 34, no. 4 (2006): 459.
2. Marshall Sahlins. "Notes on the Original Affluent Society." In *Man the Hunter*, edited by R. B. Lee and I. DeVore. New York: Aldine, 1968, 85–89.
3. Quoted from the New International Version of the Bible: James 2:5.
4. Mark Radecke. "Service-learning and the spiritual formation of college students." *Word and World* 26, no. 3 (2006): 296.
5. Ibid.
6. The legal minimum wage in the Dominican Republic depends on the size of the company and on the kind of business. For farm workers, who are among the lowest paid workers in the country, the minimum wage was equivalent to about US$4.60 a day in 2011, for a ten-hour workday. Minimum wage for sugarcane workers, many of whom are Haitian, was just under US$3 per day in 2011. Workers who are illegal are likely to receive far less. (U.S. Department of State, Bureau of Democracy, Human Rights and Labor. "Country Report in Human Rights Practices for 2011: Dominican Republic."www.state.gove/j/drl/rls/hrrpt/humanrightsreport/index.htm#wrapper. Accessed April 3, 2013.)
7. Some estimates suggest that from about 1995 through the first decade of 2000, the informal economy has been the source of more than half of nonagricultural jobs in Latin America, 75 percent in Africa, and over 40 percent in Asia. Kristina Flodman Becker. "The informal economy," Sida, Department for Infrastructure and Economic Co-operation, March 2004.http://rru.worldbank.org/Documents/PapersLinks/Sida.pdf. Accessed April 3, 2013.
8. ILO (International Labor Organization) Background Paper. "Growth, employment and social cohesion in the Dominican Republic: ILO-IMF tripartite consultation on job-rich and inclusive growth in the Dominican Republic. Santo Domingo, January 13, 2013. www.imf.org/external/country/DOM/rr/2013/013113.pdf . Accessed April 3, 2013.
9. Arturo Escobar. *Encountering Development: The Making and Unmaking of the Third World*. Princeton, NJ: Princeton University Press, 1995.
10. This reflects a process that may have accompanied the industrial revolution in Europe and elsewhere centuries earlier. Karl Polanyi. *The Great Transformation*. New York: Farrar & Rinehart, 1944.
11. Amartya Sen. *Development as Freedom*. Oxford: Oxford University Press, 1999.
12. Paul Farmer. *Pathologies of Power: Human Rights and the New War on the Poor*. Berkeley: University of California Press, 2004.
13. Michael Taylor. *Not Angels but Agencies: The Ecumenical Response to Poverty—A Primer*. Geneva: WCC Publications, 1995, 52.

Chapter Four

Bringing Religion In

About a month after my second trip to Sabaneta, I met with Chris Weichman for an interview. The Clen-Moore Church, where he is the pastor, is located in a community that is more urban and diverse than New Wilmington, about a fifteen-minute drive away. Chris had been to Sabaneta five times as well as on other short-term mission trips. Although we had spent time working together in Sabaneta over the two years of my research, this was the first time we had sat down for a formal interview. I began by telling Chris that I wanted to get a broader perspective on the trip we had just completed, a better sense of how it fit into the work of the church. He explained:

> God desires for his people to flourish. That is a good word, to flourish. My congregation may see that as financial gain and wealth. But a more biblical understanding is that when we come to faith, we are more ourselves. If you look at Genesis, God made the world in the garden of Eden, and we are separated from that perfection by sin. So the process is that there is creation, and there is sin, and the goal is to re-create the world and make it beautiful again.

Chris's remarks reminded me of a Hebrew concept, *tikkun olam*, which means "repairing the world," that undergirds much charity and development work within Judaism.

Chris shifted gears for a moment, explaining that in a recent sermon, he talked to the parish about the significance of the scholarship program that the congregation helps to fund in Sabaneta, comparing it with the GI bill, which had benefited many of his congregants after World War II. "I told them, 'The GI bill allowed you to flourish. It is the same for the Dominican kids. God desires that we flourish. God gave you gifts and talents, and wants you to use them.'" He continued, linking back to his starting point:

I think I see things differently now that I have kids. I think about what we do, as parents, to help them to flourish, to develop their gifts. . . . We are not going to do things *for* people [in Sabaneta] that they aren't able to do. It is about relationships, and helping each other to flourish. God doesn't want us, and the world, to be marred by difference and sin. The garden was good. It's not literally about Adam and Eve, but it's the metaphor—there was no enmity. That's what we want to get back to.

The faith described by Chris is a critical element of people's lives and a powerful motivator for donors and recipients of aid. Thinking about how we help others to flourish in the world and acting upon that is a way not only to express our own sentiments but to move toward creating a world based on an understanding of the sacred. In this way, faith itself can be fundamentally social, even outside of religious institutions or organizations. Faith is not separate from the choices that people make or the ways in which they make those choices.

Many people of faith take a perspective that a religious commitment is not separate from involvement in working for a more just society, often through religious communities or organizations. Mennonite churches, for example, have been very active in economic development work in the past few decades and see this focus on development work not just instrumentally, as a strategy to encourage conversion, but as part of the church's mission, regardless of whether it gets new members as a result. They emphasize that development goes beyond merely meeting material needs and includes addressing less tangible concerns for the whole person, such as human dignity and people's desire to find meaning that transcends material conditions. Consequently, development workers separate a religious approach to economic development from other approaches.[1] To repeat the language of Chris Weichman, they understand development is about allowing one another, helping one another, to flourish.

The long and deep involvement of Christians and Christian organizations in antipoverty work stems from interpretations of theology and religious teachings that deal extensively with the problems of poverty. I am not a theologian and cannot adequately offer a thorough review of the scriptural context of these questions. I happily leave that very worthwhile project to others. But some basic frameworks are frequently referenced by those directly engaged in various forms of charity, economic development, and social service work. These perspectives give us a reference point for understanding how religious service providers see the theological value of what they do and how they put their service into a context of faith, perspectives that can be useful in thinking about service work in the context of short-term missions as well.

FAITH-BASED ORGANIZATIONS

Faith-based organizations are a tremendously important part of international development work, providing services that range from disaster relief to refugee support to microcredit programs for poor rural women. Not all faith-based organizations are Christian, by any means; many organizations have been founded according to the principles of other faith traditions. Organizations that can be called "faith-based" are quite varied from one another in size, programming, their ideas about what constitutes "development," the ways in which their religious foundation influences their practice, and a number of other ways, so it is difficult to generalize about their roles and impacts. Some are very large and global in scope. World Vision, for example, is an enormous faith-based organization with programs in many countries. Others are small, sometimes working only in one country, one county, or even one congregation, school, or other organization. Some are ecumenical, while others are attached to a particular denomination or tradition. The Presbyterian Church (USA), for example, has a very active global ministries program that employs about 100 people directly, provides about $6 million a year in disaster assistance and also funds staff and grants to medical and development programs.[2]

For some organizations, providing aid to the poor is itself seen as a way to enact Christian values and show Christian love, but faith-based organizations vary in just how "faith based" they represent themselves to be. Some organizations demonstrate they are permeated with religion and others claim only a loose attachment to religious ideals. Organizations that are specifically tied to religious institutions are comfortable referencing religious principles, but when religious agencies make financial appeals to donors and congregations, they also have to show that they are nonsectarian, effective, and credible. Most researchers and others who have examined congregational social service programs find that they are not directly aimed at recruiting new members.[3] Rather, such programs spring from a sense of responsibility and a pragmatic approach to perceived needs. In the 1980s and 1990s, in order to win and retain support from both government and private sources, faith-based organizations tended to increase bureaucratic requirements, specialization, professionalization, and the diversity of their projects.

RELIGIOUS PERSPECTIVES ON ECONOMIC DEVELOPMENT

Religious individuals and organizations providing services to the poor have frequently thought not only strategically but theologically about the relationships between religion and economic development. From this perspective, the issue is not just an instrumental one of how to make people less poor, as may be the case in economic theory, but a broader one of how to bring human society more in line with a sacred vision of the world. A useful theology of development examines why Christians, as individuals and through organizations, should be concerned with poverty and development, as well as how development can be carried out from a biblical perspective.[4] Michael Taylor, who has worked in the ecumenical aid movement for many years, including as the head of the organization Christian Aid, suggests two ways to relate the Christian faith to the issue of economic development. The first starts with Christian teachings and examines how they apply to economic questions; the second looks at practical economic questions and asks how faith applies to them.[5] Either strategy is complex and may raise as many questions as it answers. But both faith and economic development have the same basic concern: to set goals in order to create positive change.[6] These theological concerns shape the ways that religious organizations approach development. Their approaches vary tremendously, but most organizations have been influenced by several broad schools of thought about the relationships between the economy and religious values.

Social Gospel

Within the United States, churches have long been involved with issues of poverty and development from a theological as well as a practical perspective. In the late nineteenth century in the United States, the discussion among Protestants about poverty was dominated by the Social Gospel movement, which fused social liberalism with a conservative theological perspective. The Social Gospel movement was not unified or particularly focused, but it encompassed a set of concerns about conditions of poverty and a call for Christians, specifically, to intervene. Organizations such as the Salvation Army, Hull House in Chicago, and other urban missions were founded in this period and focused mostly on offering humanitarian aid such as emergency food, employment bureaus, and health clinics. The movement arose largely in response to a pervasive belief that poverty was a result of individuals' shortcomings, and its proponents asserted not only that poverty and inequality were the result of societal forces, but that Christians had a responsibility to work for the transformation of the social order.[7] Social Gospel leaders tended to argue that what they saw as the desperate living conditions of the poor obstructed the poor from developing the talents and skills that would allow them to lead moral lives. An additional concern was that social injustice, as demonstrated in the plight of the poor, resulted from a failure of society to reflect the kingdom of God. Social reform was thus cast as an essential part of the work of the church to bring about God's reign on earth.

During the twentieth century, the tenets of the Social Gospel movement continued to have considerable influence on antipoverty efforts.[8] Today, mainline Protestant denominations and African American churches continue to give high priority to the reform of social institutions as well as to provide services directly to those in need.

A Theology of Liberation

A more radical emphasis on social change as a solution to poverty can be seen in the religious movement that started in Latin America in the 1960s, often referred to as liberation theology. Originating with a number of Catholic theologians, liberation theology offered a far-reaching social and political critique of Western society, capitalism, and the marginalization of the poor. One element of the teachings of prominent theologians was the assertion that the ultimate goal of Christianity was to end the suffering and oppression linked with poverty through a radical transformation of economic conditions. This movement emphasized the need to understand poverty as a theological problem, suggesting that in a world where resources are abundant, human deprivation is a sin committed against the poor by the rest of society. The duty of Christians, then, is to work against unjust social conditions. In this particular vision of economic development, improving economic conditions is a means to an end, rather than an end in itself. The goal of development is not material prosperity, but a higher quality of life for the individual, including dignity, human rights, and self-fulfillment. Poverty itself is seen as an impediment to self-fulfillment. Liberation theology advocates the transformation of society in order to provide conditions that allow individuals to live meaningful lives and communities to thrive.

Although the Catholic hierarchy largely moved away from this approach in the 1980s and 1990s, it remains influential at a grassroots level in much of the underdeveloped world and also has influenced non-Catholic organizations. It is echoed in calls for a radical transformation of the contemporary global economy by theologians like Tony Campolo, who asserts that "it's time to repent our affluence."[9] He urges Americans to reject conspicuous consumption and to "have our hearts broken" at the plight of the poor. Like liberation theology, this perspective suggests that the wealth of some is dependent on the poverty of others in ways that are fundamentally unjust. Campolo suggests that a radical commitment to a biblical Jesus creates the inability to tolerate injustice.[10] Framed in this way, the service work of individuals and congregations can become a form of cultural critique, a commentary on our relative wealth and the conditions of others.

More Conservative Approaches

A more politically conservative approach to providing social services is also prevalent in the United States, and within this approach we can identify two areas of tension. One is whether the responsibility for solving problems of poverty rests mainly with the individual or at a social level, and the other is whether churches should focus more strongly on evangelism rather than charity. Nondenominational and evangelical churches emphasize individual responsibility and personal morality rather than social and political reforms. Advocates of this more individualistic approach tend to think focusing on personal influence and individual behaviors, rather than social inequality and institutional change, is the way to solve social problems. This approach also emphasizes offering charity to the individual rather than seeking social reforms, aiming to improve the world one person at a time. In a conservative Protestant organization studied by anthropologist Erica Bornstein, for example, bringing development to the poor is understood as a Christian act. In this view, economic development has two purposes: to introduce Christian beliefs to individuals and to restore their God-given potential. [11]

In conservative circles, charity may be seen as a strategy for evangelism, merely a means to the end of religious conversion. [12] I interviewed a woman who traveled with an evangelical short-term mission group, who said:

> I think the people [in the host community], if they knew we were coming just to preach, would not have been receptive. We were coming to build a school, to help, but not just in material ways. While you were working there was more opportunity to share. I was working mostly with the children, and I tried to talk to them about God. People were more receptive that way. They saw that we were there to help, not just to shove the Bible at them.

Her sense was that service work provided both an opportunity to evangelize and a foundation for trust that made the recipients of charity more receptive to the message.

A similarly pragmatic approach suggests that people's basic needs must be met so that people can be receptive to a religious message. One pastor whom I interviewed had participated in a series of short-term mission trips to Kenya and over several years helped build a church, a Christian elementary school, and a hospital. He noted:

> The church is not the only thing that is important to a community. The entire community must be healthy and taken care of in order for the church to succeed. You can have a beautiful new church, but if the people are too sick to come to services or not educated enough to understand, then it is a waste.

Aaron Christy, the youth minister at the Clen-Moore congregation, has been on numerous mission trips, both with youth groups and on his own. He explained his understanding of short-term mission as part of "God's call to the church, to go out and to serve others." He elaborated:

It's about sacrifice of the self for the cause of the greater good. It's about making the world a better place. In my understanding of theology, the kingdom of God has come through Jesus Christ, and he said, "As my Father has sent me, so I send you." My understanding of that is that we are sent as the church, with the power of God's word, to promote social betterment. To share the gospel, to meet people's needs.

Aaron, like many others, expresses a holistic viewpoint that mission is concerned with both material and spiritual needs. He continued:

With the [short-term mission] trips, some people like to make them focus on evangelism, others make them about social needs. I like to bring both parts to it. If there is someone in dire poverty, they are not going to be able to listen [to a religious message]. But if you care for them, and show genuine love, they are more likely to listen. . . . We need to lead by example—not just to reach out locally, but to go to all the world.

Too direct a focus on charity, however, does not always resonate with more strictly evangelical approaches. A theological position that advocates giving higher priority to spiritual concerns than to worldly ones can result in an ambivalence or even animosity toward charity and development work, which can be seen as an unnecessary distraction from the "real" work of saving souls through conversion.

Religious Conversion and Economic Prosperity

In their reflections on the poverty that they encounter, short-term mission participants often remark on their perception that people in poor communities have a deeper spirituality than do those living in more comfortable circumstances, a subject that I discussed in Chapter 3. This idea has substantial roots within Christian traditions and is echoed by many religious providers of social services, both in the United States and globally. It may be particularly resonant with adherents of Pentecostalism, who strongly link prosperity with a sober lifestyle and hard work.[13] However, this notion has inherent contradictions.

On the one hand, a strong tradition links material poverty with spiritual wealth, but on the other hand, moral uprightness and the self-discipline that comes with living according to Christian principles will lead to individual prosperity.[14] For example, widespread conversion to Protestantism in Latin America in the 1980s was seen by some analysts as a choice that some families made in part because of a belief that it would help them to "get ahead" economically, and in some cases, it did so. Avoiding spending money on alcohol and gambling, for example, can free up resources for families to spend on other needs, like education or investing in work ventures. In the long run, however, analysts have observed that religious conversion does not seem to be sufficient to transform conditions of poverty. The reasons for this are complex. The case may have been overstated in the first place, either because the difference in spending patterns was too small to really change families' lifestyles or because the money "wasted" on these pursuits was exaggerated by Protestant leaders and converts. Perhaps more significantly, changing behavior patterns on the individual level did not seem to be sufficient to create opportunities for increasing income or employment in areas where there was no larger-scale economic development. Without larger-scale social efforts to alleviate poverty, religious affiliation in and of itself neither makes people poor nor creates wealth.

ECONOMIC AID AND CONGREGATIONS

Although they draw on different forms of theological inspiration, American congregations have a long tradition of helping the needy. Nearly all U.S. congregations offer some kind of social service program, some aimed at serving their own (often middle-class) members, some serving needy congregants, and others serving the wider community. A study of congregations in urban Philadelphia found that 92 percent of congregations offered some formal aid program, while another study of nonurban congregations in the Lehigh Valley of Pennsylvania found that nearly 97 percent had some social aid program. Although national data are more difficult to find, these two very thorough studies suggest that such programs are common across a large majority of congregations. [15]

Many congregations collaborate with other service providers; some churches are widely connected with other churches, secular nonprofits, and government agencies, often part of informal and formal networks. [16] Congregations also serve as important hubs that mobilize volunteers within the community and build such networks. [17] They act as caring communities that encourage shared values, long-term relationships, and emotional connectedness. Beyond such formal programs, congregations often act as centers for informal help, providing avenues of mutual emotional, material, and social support that people turn to. [18] The social service projects that emerge from short-term mission are another kind of outreach, extending economic aid beyond the congregation's own community into the sphere of global mission. Analytically, they do not fall neatly into existing categories; that is, they are not faith-based organizations in their own right, but they often transcend single congregations.

Some short-term mission programs sponsored by congregations work through established faith-based (or secular) organizations, providing financial and volunteer support to ongoing development initiatives in host communities. Accommodating short-term mission groups can present challenges for professional agencies. Sociologist Robert Wuthnow recounts an interview with a female professional development worker who said, "Everybody wants to get on a plane and go overseas and solve people's problems."[19] In her view, volunteers usually have little understanding of people's needs and of programs that actually work. She went on to suggest that the challenge is to harness the energy of volunteers without letting it interfere with professional efforts. Many faith-based organizations that work with mission groups find that these visits can be an important way for them to attract and maintain donations and long-term volunteers. A faith-based aid organization in Haiti, for example, received an influx of short-term volunteers after the catastrophic earthquake there in 2010. Although housing and feeding volunteers created logistical complications, staff felt that getting people to Haiti would dramatically increase their commitment to the Haitian people and longer-term economic development there.[20]

Most congregation-based, short-term mission projects, like the Sabaneta partnership, operate relatively independently, unconnected to other organizations, faith based or not. The Presbyterian regional liaison for the Caribbean, Jo Ella Holman, told me of various short-term groups that she sees in the Dominican Republic, estimating that thousands of missionaries visit every year from different North American churches. Although some of these groups coordinate their work through denominational programs, others work through NGOs and some through long-term missionaries. Although she believes that the resources the short-term programs bring into small Dominican communities are enormously significant, they are largely uncoordinated. Jo Ella stressed that building relationships is also critical, but acknowledged that balancing relationship building with economic assistance can be challenging. She noted: "There can be dependency issues. Some churches are very concerned about this. Others are concerned about autonomy. There are lots of power dynamics involved, as well as the issues of objectifying each other. [A partnership] has to involve a conversation about these issues." In the case of the Sabaneta partnership, team members participate in a very active and ongoing conversation that considers the best ways to improve and augment projects based on discussions between the Dominican and American partners about the needs and aspirations of the Dominican community.

The team members who travel to Sabaneta emphasize the importance of the relationships they create. They see these relationships as the most significant benefit of the partnership, as the most personally rewarding aspect of the trip, and as the one objective of mission travel that could not be accomplished in any other way. Despite the barriers of language and culture, these relationships demonstrate the authenticity of their experience, making them different from tourists, who do not have relationships, and colonial elites, who could care less about relationships. This sense of authenticity may be significant in another way: by developing authentic relationships within the context of short-term mission, participants demonstrate the authenticity of their relationships to God. Those relationships also demonstrate a faith-based social commitment; the congregation sees the service projects of volunteers as an outreach of the church.

This opportunity for dialogue is one of the strengths of congregation-based programs, church-to-church partnerships, and other short-term mission projects that allow them to operate at a more local and intimate level than larger, institutionalized NGOs and faith-based organizations. Although working at such a small scale certainly can create challenges, it also is an advantage. Short-term mission partnerships are grassroots driven and able to respond to needs, interests, and initiatives of individuals in both the sending and host community. In order to be successful, they must feel compelling to participants on both sides—people who do, after all, have limited time, money, and capacity to take on causes. Chris Weichman described how his congregation has responded to the Sabaneta partnership:

> In terms of the effects that the trip has on our church, there is a lot of interest, sustained interest, in the scholarship program. That seems to make a real difference. We see kids that finish school, that go on to college, that finish college. They need that, someone saying they believe in them, the chance to go to a good school.

Although some members of the congregation wonder if their efforts and resources would be better focused on issues of poverty in their own communities, he continued, the connection to Sabaneta has the potential to raise awareness of the needs at home as well and to help participants think about how to be fully engaged in issues of social justice not just during a one-week trip, but also during the rest of the year.

COMPASSIONATE AID

Although raising participants' awareness about social justice issues is valuable, volunteers find an immediate satisfaction in seeing, and contributing to, concrete tasks. As one man I interviewed said: "If you wanted the children to get fed, you couldn't just pray that it would happen. You had to get in the kitchen and cook for them." In a study of volunteers working in U.S. food banks, volunteers describe many motives for their work: putting skills to a positive use, having a sense of purpose and efficacy, making a positive difference in the lives of others, having a sense of teamwork, and so on.[21] Many food aid charities are attached to religious communities, and one volunteer notes that if you are working in this area to be "successful" (as in ending hunger), it will be frustrating, because there is always more need, but if you are doing it to be "faithful," then it is rewarding and you can continue.[22]

Social outreach—especially the notion that middle-class Christians should live with the poor as a way to transform their own understandings of the world[23] —is important to the progressive Christian movement. Experiencing poverty firsthand—seeing, smelling, and tasting the world that "the poor" live in—is understood as a way to gain an authentic connection between volunteers and the poor that cannot be achieved merely through reading or even watching a video or film. This notion of authenticity—in life, faith, communities, relationships, experience, one's spiritual journey—has emerged as a significant concern in contemporary American Christianity. The missional church movement urges church members to radically reimagine "mission" as the central role of any church and to engage more completely as missionaries with their own communities.[24] In this view, the "church" itself is conceptualized not as a place, but as a body of people engaged in mission—mission not just in distant places, but in the culture in which the church is located.[25] Although this goal is explicitly distinct from those of short-term mission, which involves travel to somewhere else, the efforts share a focus on mission through being present in a disadvantaged community, in order to enact, to embody, and to incarnate the faithfulness and the reign of God, demonstrating faith to those outside the church itself.[26] This notion of being present, of witnessing the lives of the poor and demonstrating solidarity with their struggles, is hardly new, having a long history in progressive Catholicism as well as in social reform movements in the nineteenth century. But it has only fairly recently become more popular within American Protestantism.

The act of being present in the lives of others is not an end in itself but is instead a way to both cultivate and demonstrate compassion. When academics and policymakers first started to examine seriously the role of NGOs in providing aid and social services globally, there was a fair amount of attention to and enthusiasm for the notion that these aid organizations were more altruistic than government agencies, that employees were motivated by a stronger sense of purpose, that they were more compassionate in their outlook and responsive to the populations they served. This enchantment with NGOs largely wore off—perhaps because over time, the organizations themselves tended to become more bureaucratized and professionalized, or perhaps because this was an overly idealistic outlook all along. But the same altruistic attitudes are now sometimes attributed to faith-based organizations and initiatives. Robert Wuthnow, for example, credits faith-based organizations with putting into practice teachings about unconditional love.[27]

As may have been the case with NGOs, claims that faith-based projects are at least potentially more effective than secular ones may be overly optimistic and risk overgeneralizing about their internal dynamics, motivations, and practice. But I see value in the willingness and ability of faith-based projects to take love seriously. Engaging in compassion as a conscious methodology, that is, engaging seriously with love—with what it means and what it requires of us individually and collectively—leads to approaching development in different ways that may be more sensitive to the needs and desires of those being served.

Many Americans have a sense that the world's problems, brought to us continually by the media, are too large and too far away for us to even imagine how to really address them. In order to begin to act, it may be necessary to think of problems of poverty not on a global scale but on a human scale. The popularity of child-sponsorship programs, for example, can be seen as one bit of evidence for this. I can't save masses of starving children, but I can reach one other person. Kristen Long, one of the medical providers who traveled to Sabaneta, said: "I look at the Bible very simply. Jesus loved everyone. We are supposed to do the same thing." She explained that for her, handing out even simple medications in the clinics can be understood as an act of compassion. Faith and compassion are evident in small deeds, in daily acts, in the ways that we approach suffering in the world.

The compassion of volunteers for those whom they seek to help does make a difference in how projects are received. Although there has been very little systematic study of the impact, economic and noneconomic, of mission volunteering on the host community,[28] a sympathetic and sophisticated article about American missionaries in Trinidad suggested that for people in the host community, the willingness of volunteers to come to the community and work alongside local people did humanize the Americans.[29] In this case, the symbolic significance of this act of participation and solidarity was much more meaningful than its economic value.

Similarly, Jerry Bruck recounted one of his experiences while working in a woman's house in the community:

> We really couldn't talk to the people we were helping, the people whose homes we were in [because no one in the construction group spoke much Spanish]. We only got little bits and pieces of their story. You could tell they were trying to speak in simple words, but it didn't matter. We couldn't acknowledge their situation, or ask about their family, their children. We just had to acknowledge they were there. There was only one person could speak enough English to converse a little. She asked me, are you one of the doctors? No, I said, I'm an engineer. She said, "Engineers don't do what you're doing—they stand back and tell people what to do!" She was impressed that she had an engineer working on her floor.

In the work that volunteers do as part of short-term missions, faith is evident in small deeds. Acts of faithful service to others are like planting a seed, often taking time and patience to see results. The work done by volunteers—

feeding children, supporting a young man's education, encouraging the dreams of others—will not ease all suffering, will not create perfection in the world, and will not make headlines, but they do bring compassion and mercy to those involved. The goodness inherent in service may both help to explain why churches continue to engage in it and why it is worthwhile to continue to work on antipoverty programs in the context of global poverty.

IS COMPASSION ENOUGH?

Serving others is fulfilling for volunteers, but the main goal of service is helping others, not experiencing personal satisfaction. In a discussion about the value of short-term mission, Chris Weichman said:

> It's hard for Americans to go and not *do* something. And so lots of times we go, and we do something bad, something that ends up being negative. We create dependency. It's easier to have something to focus on. Sometimes "doing" is a defense mechanism; we don't know how to talk to people who are different. But what is the bridge? If you scrap the projects, how do you connect people to people?

The satisfaction that comes from volunteer work and from giving can distract the volunteer from understanding the deeper problems at the root of poverty. In an interview, Jo Ella Holman, the Presbyterian regional liaison for the Caribbean, praised the work of short-term mission volunteers but raised an important concern, saying: "The medical part—it is treating the symptoms. Not that it isn't important, but it doesn't get to the root problems. Is it that people don't have the money for treatment, or is it that high-quality treatment isn't available? And why?" Jo Ella is not the only one to raise such a concern. In the study of U.S. food banks that I discussed briefly earlier, sociologist Jane Poppendieck suggests that while emergency food aid represents an outpouring of compassion and energizes hordes of volunteers who make the system run, the need for such charity is both a symptom and a cause of society's failure to deal with rising inequality and an inadequate welfare system. It is a symptom of a need that exists because we have turned from solving problems to managing them; it is a cause because reducing moral discomfort with poverty permits participants to feel as though they have done something.[30] This culture of charity makes poverty seem like a normal part of social life, rather than something that should be surprising or exceptional, and also makes personal generosity, rather than social transformation, seem like an effective response.

Poppendieck notes that many food providers are unwilling to deprive the poor of aid but are very aware of the limits to their work in solving underly-

ing problems. Short-term mission participants certainly share similar concerns. One college student I interviewed said:

> I, well, I don't want to say that what we did wasn't worth it, it was definitely
> worth it. But it doesn't get at the real problems. Like, you give them vitamins,
> and they might have vitamins for a month, but then what? Or there were a lot
> of kids we treated for worms. So you treat them for a month, and then they are
> better for a month, but they are drinking the same water and walking around
> barefoot. They're just going to get them again.

Poppendieck suggests that the joys and demands of charity work divert us,
socially and individually, from seeking more fundamental solutions.[31] Prac-
ticing charity is also easier than creating fundamental change, which requires
advocacy and empowerment. Yet such work is not only daunting, but can
also alienate donors, overextend staff, and provide less satisfying experiences
for volunteers,[32] rather than making a perceptible difference.

Another problem with acts of charity, such as working in a soup kitchen
or a short-term mission project, is that they represent what is essentially a
one-way relationship, ones whose ideal form is that of a generous donor and
a grateful recipient. It is asymmetrical in terms of power. The donor has the
power to give or to withhold, to decide what the gift consists of, and to create
the terms of the gift. The recipient has only one choice—to accept the gift or
not. And, depending on the situation, this may not really be a choice at all. In
this relationship of giver and receiver, the "giver" sees need as the defining
characteristic of the person who is receiving. Charity is not something that
we offer to those whom we see as our equals.[33] Charity tends to emphasize
the differences between the donor and recipient rather than things they have
in common.

RECIPROCITY

The one-sided nature of charity is a good and necessary part of human
relationships. Each of us can imagine a crisis that might leave us dependent
on the goodwill of others—a natural disaster, an emergency. And we can
imagine wanting to reach out to others who are in such need. We don't only
have to imagine. Every time the media portray a crisis or disaster, help pours
in, sometimes in the form of donations and sometimes in the form of volunteers. Charity is a way for us to express our desire to help others, to express
human connections, even with those we don't know. This value is fundamental not just to Christianity but to all of the world's major religions.

But it remains a lopsided transaction. When charity is the basis of an
ongoing relationship, it can distort the relationship between donor and recipient, creating dependency, resentment, and suspicion, often on both sides.

Donors may feel that their gifts are not appreciated or used properly, that they are being taken advantage of, or that they are being cheated. Recipients may feel denigrated, misunderstood, or embarrassed. Aid givers may be viewed by a community as paternalistic or ineffective. And although visitors may attach a great deal of emotional importance to their encounters, recipients of projects may find them less meaningful, particularly in communities that frequently host volunteers. These challenges are familiar to those working in international aid and human services. Jo Ella Holman noted that many congregational partnerships find they need to address this issue:

> What most partnerships struggle with is how to balance the financial part with the relational part. Whether it's churches or anything, if they are coming to give money, they see the people as "charity objects." With the church, the goal is relationships, friendships that give testimony to a unity in Christ. So the money part is difficult.

A better goal, she suggested, is to try to create more balanced relationships.

Although Christian giving, including service work, is based on an ideal of unconditional love, volunteers do have expectations of recipients. Indeed, sociologist Robert Wuthnow notes that our culture celebrates the role of those who give, but the role or obligation of recipients is less well defined, ranging from expressing gratitude to repaying the "gift," to accepting aid with a feeling of shame.[34] Although full-time aid workers are trained to deal with these expectations, volunteers generally are not. A challenge, then, that short-term missions and other aid efforts face is creating a more equitable relationship between partners who have different access to resources and power.[35]

One way to create balance is to rethink the relationships between those who give and those who receive. Rather than expressing charity, an essentially one-way exchange, another model is to practice reciprocity. Reciprocity is an exchange of gifts in which both parties have the opportunity to give and to receive. Anthropologists who study small-scale traditional societies observe the importance of reciprocity in managing social relationships. Giving a gift demonstrates regard for a partner and cements a relationship. A gift, of course, may not always be immediately returned but does create an expectation that someday the giver will receive a gift in return. In traditional societies, the relationships created by reciprocity can be the basis for managing trade networks over long distances as well as the expression of friendship and love in close relationships. In our own society, we engage in reciprocity all the time—in literal exchanges of gifts at birthdays and holidays, but also by doing favors for friends, helping coworkers with tasks, or managing carpooling in a neighborhood.

When I talk about reciprocity to my students, it sometimes makes them uncomfortable to think that the gifts they give to family and friends can be seen as creating obligations and expectations of return. The idea that one expects a gift in return seems mercenary and is at odds with a cultural emphasis on giving generously. But reciprocity does imply an obligation—not that the recipient will immediately hand over a gift of equal value, but that a relationship has been created that both parties can depend on when they need it. Within the framework of reciprocity, the gift itself is not important, but the relationship that is symbolized through the gift and the act of giving is. Framed in that way, the obligation for return is put into a different light. In a gift of charity, the giver does not expect a return, and the relationship is one dimensional; in an act of reciprocity, the recipient has an obligation to return, and the relationship extends over time. The expectation of return creates a relationship based on equality, rather than a power imbalance. Charity excuses the recipient from the obligation to repay, a normal component of reciprocity, which is fundamental to social life.[36]

Short-term missions may be fulfilling, because they allow participants to experience giving not in an abstract way, as with writing a check for a good cause, but in a deeply experiential setting, in the context of personal relationships. Giving also presents the central challenge of short-term mission, however. How can the obligations of reciprocity be returned by people in the host community in order to create and maintain balanced relationships?

Resolving these issues is challenging and may be a matter of reshaping participants' perceptions and expectations rather than through enacting any specific changes in the ways projects are organized or services delivered. Short-term mission participants are often acutely aware of feeling that they gain tremendous rewards from their experiences. A college student participant expressed this to me, saying: "It was a great opportunity, and I want to go back. It helped *me* as a person maybe more than I helped anyone else." One of the participants in Sabaneta said, "I get so much out of this trip—and *I'm* the one that's supposed to be giving." Encouraging volunteers to reflect on what they gain from the experience can be a way to develop a sense of reciprocity as part of short-term mission. Studies of other kinds of service and volunteer work clearly encourage self-reflection as a key to learning from experience. Educators Robert Rhoads and Julie Neurerer conducted a study of a college service-learning trip to Guatemala.[37] Although this trip was secular, the students engaged in many of the same activities as most mission groups—working and building relationships in a poor community. Rhoads and Neurerer focus on mutuality of service—that through service, one both gives and receives. Developing an awareness of this mutuality is an important part of the individual growth of participants. For this to be fully expressed, they suggest that simply reflecting on these gains greatly enhances students' awareness of it.

SHORT-TERM MISSIONARIES

As religious organizations, and the individuals who are a part of them, work in service of the poor, the projects they undertake resemble those that are offered by secular agencies—providing social services, working on local infrastructure, and improving living conditions. The differences between religious service providers and volunteers and their secular counterparts are in their motivations for doing this kind of work and the ways in which they envision the meanings of this work. At times, as I have talked to people involved in short-term mission work, the idea of "mission" has seemed, to me, nearly synonymous with the idea of "service." Although members of the Sabaneta team frequently reflect on what it means to be a missionary, they rarely use the word "missionaries" to describe themselves. At one of the orientation sessions, Chris Weichman noted that the team does not go to Sabaneta to evangelize, pointing out that the role of the team is to help the Dominican church in its mission to serve its neighbors. Like other team members, he expresses some discomfort with the term missionary, with its implication of religious conversion, and with some of the historical baggage that it seems to convey. Chris said to me: "Cancu calls us missionaries, insists on it really. I don't like that. *Missionaries* is really such a loaded term. Isn't it better to say 'partners, friends, colleagues, brothers and sisters in Christ'—any of those?" The team leaders use these terms in English and also use the word *hermandad*—"brotherhood"—in Spanish to refer to the partnership, even though people in the Dominican church and in the larger community frequently do use the term *missionaries* to refer to the group.

Ralph Hawkins discussed the idea of mission, indicating, "We are there to learn from them." He continued, "This is not the old model of missionaries, which was that there was the 'West' and 'the rest,'" setting these terms apart with dramatic quotation marks in the air. "God is alive and well in the Dominican Republic. It is a blessing to learn from them. Mission happens from everywhere to everywhere. It is reciprocal." His definition of "mission" here is expansive and refers not to a conversion of faith but to the act of service itself and to the compassion that it both demonstrates and instills. Service becomes a way to enact compassion, to literally care for others. Chris said to me: "We don't want to turn people into Christian mission tourists. But we do want people to come back, and think, I went where people are really poor, and how does that affect how I read the Bible?" Being in a culturally unfamiliar setting encourages participants to set aside or circumvent activities and attitudes that may act as a barrier to attitudes of caring for others at home.

The projects that congregations engage in through short-term mission and direct partnerships are immediate and concrete, and that allows them to connect global issues, like poverty, to parishioners' own experiences. By working directly with individuals in other parts of the world through short-term mission trips, the desire to help others becomes an immediate possibility and gives church members a sense that they have a personal stake in the outcome. Mission trips thus offer opportunities for both global engagement and personal enrichment. The direct connections they create between individuals in different regions allow people in one location to feel that they have an impact on individuals in another, which is—or potentially can be—transformative not only for the North American participants but also for the communities they visit. Poverty is understood as not merely an economic problem but also a theological one, and the solutions to the problems of poverty thus need to be more than just material. They encompass how people listen to and understand one another as part of a larger religious community. Moving toward reciprocity, rather than charity, can be a way to create projects that develop social justice, which includes strategies that reduce inequities and ultimately make charity less necessary.

NOTES

1. Richard A. Yoder, Calvin W. Redekop, and Vernon E. Jantzi. *Development to a Different Drummer: Anabaptist/Mennonite Experiences and Perspectives.* Intercourse, PA: Good Books, 2004, 296.

2. Robert Wuthnow. *Boundless Faith: The Global Outreach of American Churches.* Berkeley: University of California Press, 2009, 127.

3. Ram A. Cnaan. *The Other Philadelphia Story: How Local Congregations Support Quality of Life in America.* Philadelphia: University of Pennsylvania Press, 2006, 101.

4. Vinay Samuel and Chris Sugden. "Theology of development." In *Evangelicals and Development: Towards a Theology of Social Change,* edited by Ronald J. Sider. Philadelphia: Westminster Press, 1982, 19.

5. Michael Taylor. *Not Angels but Agencies: The Ecumenical Response to Poverty—A Primer.* Geneva: WCC Publications, 1995, 118–123.

6. Ibid., 128.

7. Julie Adkins, Laurie Occhipinti, and Tara Hefferan. *Not By Faith Alone: Social Services, Social Justice, and Faith-Based Organizations in the U.S.* Lanham, MD: Lexington Books, 2010.

8. Few providers of social services today would describe themselves as part of a Social Gospel movement, which is more important in terms of its historic influence than as a current idea.

9. Tony Campolo. "Challenging the church with missions." In *The Short Term Missions Boom: A Guide to International and Domestic Involvement,* edited by Michael J. Anthony. Grand Rapids, MI: Baker Books, 1994, 21.

10. Ibid., 23.

11. Erica Bornstein. *The Spirit of Development: Protestant NGOs, Morality, and Economics in Zimbabwe.* New York: Routledge, 2003, 48.

12. Omri Elisha. *Moral Ambition: Mobilization and Social Outreach in Evangelical Megachurches.* Berkeley: University of California Press, 2011, 8.

13. Gregory Deacon. "Pentecostalism and development in Kibera Informal Settlement, Nairobi." *Development in Practice* 22, no. 5–6 (2012): 663–674.

14. As I write this book, a "prosperity gospel" is enjoying significant popularity in the United States, but here I refer more to the notions of Calvinism and the Reformation.

15. Cnaan, 78; Robert Wuthnow. *Saving America? Faith-Based Service and the Future of Civil Society.* Princeton, NJ: Princeton University Press, 2004.

16. Cnaan, 58–59.

17. Ibid., 62.

18. Ibid., 63–75.

19. Wuthnow, *Saving America?*, 129.

20. Tara Hefferan, "The meaning of suffering: Short-term missionaries in post-earthquake Haiti." Paper presented at the annual meeting for the American Anthropological Association, New Orleans, Louisiana, November 17–21, 2010.

21. Janet Poppendieck. *Sweet Charity? Emergency Food and the End of Entitlement.* New York: Penguin, 1998, 200.

22. Ibid., 193.

23. Robert P. Jones, *Progressive and Religious.* Lanham, MD: Rowman & Littlefield, 2008, 95.

24. Darrell L. Guder, ed. *Missional Church: A Vision for the Sending of the Church in North America.* Grand Rapids, MI: Eerdmans, 1998.

25. Ibid., 80–81.

26. Ibid., 129, 135.

27. Wuthnow, *Saving America?*, 256.

28. In fact some of these studies were done by researchers who were studying other topics in a community that happened to receive mission groups. A more systematic study of a host community is Robert Priest's "Peruvian churches acquire linking social capital through short-term mission partnerships." *Journal of Latin American Theology: Reflections from the Global South* 2 (2007): 175–189.

29. Kevin Birth, "What is your mission here?: A Trinidadian perspective on visits from the 'Church of Disneyworld.'" *Missiology* 34, no. 4 (2006): 497–508.

30. Poppendieck, 5.

31. Ibid., 19.

32. Ibid., 268–276.

33. Ibid., 254.

34. Wuthnow, *Saving America?*, 260.

35. Ibid., 247.

36. Poppendieck, 251.

37. Robert A. Rhoads and Julie Neurerer. "Alternative spring break: Learning through community service." *NASPA Journal* 35, no. 2 (1998): 100–118.

Chapter Five

Getting Practical

Broad theoretical approaches explain poverty on a global scale and can provide a foundation for thinking about ways to create more equitable systems. But how do they apply to "actually getting things done"—acting on a human scale in order to better the lives of individuals, families, and communities? The work of human development "in the trenches" may not seem to produce enormous, world-changing transformations, but it can produce visible, tangible improvements in people's daily lives. It creates the drops of water that individually are nearly invisible but collectively make up the sea.

Governmental and nongovernmental programs and agencies have been working at this human level for decades, sometimes successfully and sometimes less so. This chapter looks at some of the strategies they use and how successful approaches can be and have been incorporated into the service work of short-term missions.

GIVE A MAN A FISH

There is an old saying, "Give a man a fish, he'll eat for a day. Teach a man to fish, he'll eat for a lifetime." The message is a reflection on the limitations of charity, a call to develop skills and capacity in order to provide long-term solutions rather than merely applying bandages. The fishing metaphor provides a jumping-off point for thinking about the kinds of concrete development projects that are undertaken in order to ameliorate poverty.

Many antipoverty initiatives are designed to transfer goods or services to meet an immediate need. Whether this approach takes the form of distributing tents and blankets to refugees, hosting a soup kitchen in a poor urban community, or providing a month's worth of pills to treat a chronic illness, it provides immediate assistance to a needy person. This is "giving a fish." We all feel compelled to give a fish sometimes, as human decency and compassion require us to reach out to those in need. And most short-term mission service work seems to fall into this category—providing staff support in orphanages, holding medical clinics in poor neighborhoods, or providing meals or clothing in an underprivileged community. According to the theories of development discussed in Chapter 3, this is a charity model. This kind of work, while essential at a human level, does not change conditions of poverty. The statement "Give a man a fish and he will eat for a day" is accurate. Before you can teach people to fish, they have to be physically well and able to learn. Simple charity addresses immediate needs but does not do anything to change that person's position tomorrow, when he will need another fish.

Another kind of initiative focuses on building capacity—emphasizing education, establishing self-help programs, and improving public health. These capacity-building projects "teach a man to fish" by providing tools and support that allow men and women to develop knowledge and skills they need in order to make a living in the hopes of reducing their dependency on charity over the long term. Based on a human development approach, such programs often not only offer academic or vocational education but also give thought to other needs—such as childcare, health, transportation, or security—that may contribute to a person's ability to be productive. Capacity-building projects can include creating and maintaining schools or educational programs for children and adults, supporting health clinics, or training adults in marketable skills. I have seen one program in rural Africa that purchased bicycles for use by community members so they could commute to work or school and then also trained several local men as bicycle mechanics. Some short-term mission projects work at this level. In Sabaneta, for example, the Pennsylvania churches provide scholarship support that allows individuals to get a good education, with the long-term goal of benefiting not only the individual but the community as well, because individuals will then be able to help others around them. "Teaching a man to fish" means that he not only can provide for his own needs in the future, but can then teach others himself. A capacity-building approach requires a longer-term commitment in recognition that these results are not immediate but rather accumulate over time.

A third type of initiative aims at the development of sustainable economic systems. Since the early 1990s, there has been a dramatic shift in thinking among theorists and practitioners of economic development that has led them to increasingly recognize the role of local people not as the "targets" of development projects but as knowledgeable people who can and should be included in the decision-making process. This approach deliberately turns that fishing metaphor on its head and "asks a man how to fish." The metaphor of "teaching" people to fish assumes that they lack basic knowledge and skills. This model questions that assumption and recognizes that individuals—including the poor—already have skills and knowledge and are competent individuals. Poverty may be caused by their inability to access the resources they need in order to use those skills. In this view, poverty may also be worsened, or even caused, by programs that are inappropriate to local circumstances. By "asking" someone how to fish, this approach encourages outsiders to bring their resources to bear on issues and in directions that are identified by the people they are trying to help. This corresponds to a social justice approach, and although it often includes the same *kinds* of initiatives and projects as a capacity-building approach, it differs in that one goal is to turn control of those projects over to the local community. The focus is on the autonomy and self-determination of poor individuals and communities, turning over control and recognizing that "solutions" to issues of poverty depend on the context of geography and culture. It leads outside organizations to offer their resources to support development projects that are identified as important by the local community, to demonstrate that they respect local knowledge and skills, and to build on local resources and culture. These projects may not change the underlying causes of poverty, but they endeavor to devise ways in which poor people can create more productive, sustainable, and rewarding lives with limited resources. In contrast to a more paternalistic approach in which the "helpers" assume they have superior knowledge or abilities, this approach values the skills and knowledge, as well as the dignity, of those being "helped."

This approach is less common for short-term mission work, but those based on a partnership model may come close to working in this way. Again, I can point to the Sabaneta partnership for an example. To the greatest extent possible, the Pennsylvania partners accept that the Dominican church should establish the priorities of the partnership—where the team goes, which homebound patients need to be seen, and what kinds of projects are most important. To be sure, this control is limited by both resources and the skills and the availability of the American travelers, but the North Americans make a genuine effort to listen to and respect the priorities of the Dominican church, to ask what their goals are, and to work toward those goals. This approach recognizes that people in the host community have skills and resources and that a good project respects and builds on those.

A final approach stretches the fishing metaphor even further, asking, "Who wants to eat fish, anyway, if there is other food out there?" Recognizing that global social and economic systems are inherently unequal, this approach challenges assumptions and promotes more transformative change. Translating this recognition into pragmatic terms often leads to projects that develop relationships across social, economic, and political boundaries, promoting social networks and confronting unjust systems. More often, this approach is an ideal rather than a practice, but developing grassroots networks that can advocate for fair government policies, ensure human rights, and promote transparency and equality can be critical in creating conditions that allow individuals, families, and communities to thrive. Historically, as well as across the world today, churches and religious institutions have provided crucial organizational and moral support to such movements. At their best, churches have given a voice precisely to the "least of these," supporting those who may be most disenfranchised. Although short-term mission groups and their sponsoring congregations may not always see themselves as engaged in policy work or political advocacy, mission trips themselves bridge many kinds of boundaries, creating new transnational grassroots networks.

Dividing projects into these types may help us think about the goals of an initiative and how it can meet those goals. The metaphor presented at the beginning of this chapter, of teaching a person to fish, provides an intuitive illustration of different approaches to antipoverty work, yet it also suggests a hierarchy of kinds of aid—that certain approaches are always preferable to others. As Michael Taylor, director of Christian Aid, an ecumenical organization, points out:

> The ecumenical family should be unapologetic about offering relief or "aid" to people who will live and die long before the systems which create the emergencies and keep people poor are changed. This immediate response to human need is easily thrown on the defensive. It can be criticized for dealing with symptoms and not causes, for changing nothing and for being a fairly cheap way by which the better-off can assuage their consciences. All of this may be true. But it is not the whole truth, and it does not remove the need or the duty to feed the hungry today and not tomorrow. Such compassion, often costly and courageous, cannot automatically be dismissed as mere charity.[1]

As Taylor suggests, charity, or giving a fish, is an essential component of meeting the needs of impoverished populations. In fact, any one organization may have any number of projects that fit under different categories as it tries to accomplish a range of goals and serve a variety of needs. Poverty is a complex and multifaceted problem, and many, if not most, organizations working to ameliorate poverty take a holistic approach.

NUTS AND BOLTS

Eventually, defining priorities and approaches gives way to the actual work of addressing issues of poverty, which happens on a human scale, on a daily level, and one person, one family, one community at a time. Antipoverty organizations implement projects with specific goals that address specific needs. The question "What kind of project should we pursue?" does not have a "one-size-fits-all" answer. Mission groups, like other aid organizations, can and do take on a number of different kinds of projects.

What to Do?

One of the first questions that needs to be addressed by any group wanting to provide aid is what kind of projects to pursue. Here, the experience of non-profit organizations may be helpful. In the 1980s and 1990s, there was a burst of enthusiasm for NGOs. Small, nonprofit organizations, the reasoning went, could connect more effectively than governments with local communities and their needs, could use money more efficiently, and were more responsive to changing circumstances on the ground. A great deal of funding began to be channeled through NGOs, which proliferated around the globe. In the following decades, NGOs have proven reasonably effective at creating and implementing development projects. They have made great strides in providing emergency aid, creating community development, improving living conditions, and sponsoring an array of projects. They also have been shown to have some limitations: they cannot improve large-scale infrastructure, like roads or bridges; and they cannot change structural conditions, like the unemployment rate or inflation. Those kinds of projects require government action. NGOs are also often limited by the kinds of funding they can obtain. Money to build a clinic, for example, is easier to find than financial support that will pay a doctor's salary.

In choosing projects, NGOs usually take one of two paths. The first, preferable, strategy is to work with a community, determine community needs, and then seek out the funding that is needed to implement a project to address those needs. A second strategy is to look at what donors are interested in funding and develop a local project that can take advantage of the resources that are being offered. Although the first strategy is more immediately responsive to the community, the second approach is pragmatic and can augment ongoing work. In choosing projects, most successful NGOs also give consideration to their own internal resources—staff expertise, time and energy of staff and volunteers, and available equipment and supplemental funding. Some NGOs focus very narrowly on specific issues, such as health care or education, while others serve a community's needs more holistically.

Short-term mission groups must balance concerns similar to those faced by NGOs. Although these groups only rarely—if ever—seek out funding beyond the sponsoring congregation, their denomination, or individually solicited donations, they must also balance the needs and desires of the host communities with what they can accomplish in practical terms. Just as NGOs balance community needs with funding opportunities, short-term mission groups must balance community needs with the availability of volunteers with specialized skills and, in many cases, funding. In Sabaneta, for example, the congregation leaders have expressed a need for a dentist to accompany the medical team. Although a dentist sometimes volunteers, most years it doesn't happen, leaving the team unable to provide dental care even though it is highly desired.

No single "type" of project is perfect. Short-term problems, such as a natural disaster, can be addressed by short-term solutions, such as distributing blankets. The same efforts don't work to help with long-term problems, which need long-term approaches. In any case, budget, personal skills and interests, and the needs and desires of the host community are some of the issues that should be considered when determining the kinds of projects a group would like to implement.

Another consideration is the scope of the project. Size matters—the size of the sponsoring congregation as well as the size of the traveling group. Larger groups and congregations may be able to mobilize a larger budget, which may allow for a greater diversity of projects. They may also have a larger pool of potential volunteers, with a greater variety of professional skills and interests. A larger traveling group does lend more hands to service projects, but this also means that projects need to employ a larger number of volunteers in meaningful work, which can present its own challenges. And although more volunteers bring the potential of doing more work, the size of the group makes a significant difference in terms of logistics within the host country. Everything from lodging to moving people to a work site can become more challenging for both project organizers and local hosts. In a larger group, volunteers may find that they spend more time with one another and have fewer opportunities to interact with their local hosts on an individual level, particularly if there are language barriers that require translators.

By their very nature, short-term mission trips mean that many volunteers are available for an intense period of time, and then the traveling group has limited contact with the host community for a long stretch of time. Project planners need to think about how a project will function once the travelers return home. Ongoing projects, such as a microcredit program, nearly always require someone in the host community to manage them; coordinating such activities with ongoing local projects and organizations can be an effective strategy to maintain a community presence in between mission visits.

Where to Go?

Another question that planners need to address at the outset is what the destination of the short-term mission will be. In my interviews with mission participants and congregational leaders, I have been struck by the number of times that I have been told that a short-term mission goes to a specific region or community because someone in the congregation had a personal tie there. Sometimes an individual made a connection through a professional link, and sometimes he or she had visited as a tourist, on a different mission trip, or in some other capacity. Occasionally the tie is through a family member. In any case, through some experience, an individual developed a passionate connection to an area, felt a strong desire to make a difference, and organized or advocated a trip to that region.

This is not a bad system. Personal interest and passion may be necessary to mobilize a short-term mission group. An enthusiastic individual may provide strong leadership and the catalyst that is needed. The personal connection also may infuse a trip with a sense of meaning and a basis for creating relationships in the host community. Building on one person's passion also carries a risk, however. If that individual ceases to be involved, for any of a host of reasons, or loses the enthusiasm he or she started with, the connection might be lost and the project would falter. Fortunately, this is not inevitable; groups can successfully establish a connection that lasts after the "founder" is gone. A successfully institutionalized connection can be even more sustainable and stronger if it is not "filtered" through just one person.

Choosing a region that someone has a connection with may have unintended side effects. Some host regions, such as Juarez, Mexico, receive many American mission teams, while others, in more remote or inaccessible locations, receive none at all. In economic development, this inequality is sometimes called the "side-of-the-road" syndrome: communities may receive disproportionate aid because they are accessible and visible. When I was working in a small indigenous community in a very remote area, for example, an NGO that served the community received a grant to build a small community center, a building that could theoretically function as a meeting place. Like other community centers in the region, the building would be small, perhaps ten by twenty feet, with a metal roof and no amenities. In other communities, this type building often served as a storage space for equipment or supplies for development projects rather than as meeting spaces. Meetings were usually held outside because of the building's small size and because the metal roof would make the inside unbearably hot during the day. As the villagers discussed the placement of the center, one of the NGO workers rose to express her opinion. "You need to put it so that it can be seen from the road," she declared. The road was about a half a mile from the cluster of houses in the village, separated from the houses by thick, thorny brush. "The government officials won't get out of their car and walk in to the village. You want them to see it, so they know you are here." In her opinion, making the village visible and demonstrating that they could complete projects like the community center, so more aid would be forthcoming in this truly impoverished community, was one of the key objectives of building the community center, more important than its ostensible function. The politically astute villagers agreed with her rationale, and the building was constructed on the road. Short-term mission teams, like government officials, may be subject to this kind of side-of-the-road bias, not venturing deeper into the brush, where the need might be more profound. This bias can be literally based on distance and ease of travel; more mission teams travel to Central America and northern South America, for example, than to sub-Saharan Africa, Southeast Asia, or other far-off regions, despite the more intense poverty—and rapid growth of Christianity—in many of those regions. Side-of-the-road bias may also be metaphoric, a *sense* of cultural distance and relative unfamiliarity; it can take as many (or more) hours to travel to parts of Brazil, for example, as it takes to arrive in the capital of Ghana, but for some travelers, a sense of familiarity with Latin America may make it seem more possible to go there than to Africa. More accessible locations certainly do have genuine needs, but it is important to recognize how these kinds of choices are made and what criteria are being used.

How would a congregation find a location without a personal connection? Some congregations work through their denomination, which has institutional ties with churches in different parts of the world as well as with nonprofit organizations. Some congregations may work through one of the many U.S.-based organizations that facilitate mission trips by providing logistical support and arrangements in a host community. In this case, congregations may find it worthwhile to make sure the organization has legal status as a nonprofit in the country in which it operates. Leaders may face a more difficult challenge in assessing the degree to which a nonprofit is integrated into the community in which it works. Some have a long-term presence and are able to effectively work in a community, while others may not be accepted by the communities in which they are located or may not understand the needs and desires of the local community.

A somewhat distinct issue about choosing a location for mission travel is that mission teams can sometimes feel alienated from a host community by the realization that their group may be just one among many in a region. The relationships team members have with their local hosts may feel emotionally profound and deep to them, and some participants may find it disorienting to realize that those local hosts have numerous other relationships and are not as emotionally connected to the team as team members feel. Participants may even wonder if they are being taken advantage of when they discover that a local community can draw on other outside groups for resources. Mission groups need to recognize that local communities and leaders are working to better their own conditions, and sometimes this can be accomplished through drawing on a number of different outside sources—NGOs, government funding, mission groups—that can each provide a different piece. Just as one mission group could never meet all of the needs of a community, a community must seek out support from a range of sources.

Defining Issues and Setting Limits

In responding to the expressed needs of a community partner, mission committees, mission teams, and team members as individuals may encounter multiple demands. Balancing these requests for support, favors, and time and resources with the resources that are actually available as well as with the desires, skills, and interests of the mission team can be an enormous challenge. Although we may recognize in the abstract that we can't do everything, in practice, saying no can be an incredible challenge.

One way to deal with this inevitable pressure is to define what the team is doing, and, through that definition, what it is not doing. Without clear criteria, team members and leaders may feel vulnerable to different kinds of pressures, both internal and external. A clear sense of "mission"—in a strategic, rather than religious sense—allows groups to focus their work on shared goals. But again, this is easier said than done. And one of the advantages to this kind of project is that it is not bureaucratized, that participants can respond to specific needs, to unanticipated circumstances, and to needs that are "off the books." When the team was in Sabaneta, for example, a local woman needed a caesarian section, and team members were asked if they could contribute a modest sum for her treatment. Twenty-five Americans obviously cannot provide financial support for all of the needs in Sabaneta, and surely many, many such circumstances exist in which aid is needed, is legitimate, and could make a huge difference. A formal NGO might not be able to respond to such a plea, constrained by internal rules and by a desire to be consistent and transparent. The team responded—not formally as an organization, but as individuals. This represented a good compromise, allowing team members to respond compassionately to an urgent request for help. Of course, the questions of what happens when the team isn't there, and how their work supports the creation of systems that provide care to those who need it, remain.

PROJECTS

As teams examine their options for providing service to others, they may find it useful to think in terms of projects that they can undertake. A development "project" is a specific initiative, usually with a limited goal and a specific timeframe. A project that has a clear beginning and ending—building a school, for example—usually is completed with the idea that its effects will last after the project itself is completed. Other projects may be ongoing—providing meals at a soup kitchen, for example—but even these "permanent" programs usually operate with an annual budget for purposes of planning.

Projects can be challenging to plan and to implement. The input and cooperation of many people may be required, logistical details must be worked out, and of course, projects nearly always need some funding. No matter what the project is, taking steps to help plan, manage, and follow up on an idea gives it a better chance of meeting its goals.[2] Attention to each of these stages can be helpful, if not essential, in carrying out good development work. Organizers can easily get absorbed in project structure and logistical details, losing track of the reasons the project is important. Focusing on the process of a project, including following up on its outcomes, allows organizers to keep some perspective on their work.

Every project has essential components. It starts with a concept or idea—what is actually going to happen and why. It needs an organizational structure that facilitates the logistics of implementing the concept. It has a project team—people actually managing and carrying out the project. These may include organizational staff, volunteers, and local participants involved in the decision-making process. A project has desired goals or outcomes, which can be short or long term. All of these components are always present, although they are sometimes implicit rather than explicit.

Projects also generally have what we think of as a target population—people whom the project is intended to reach. Some projects are aimed at "the poorest of the poor"—those who are most marginalized, with fewest resources. Others may be directed at a segment of the population—children in a neighborhood, women who belong to a church, or unemployed men. Some projects, such as a new water filtration system or a community center building, may be intended to benefit a community more broadly.

What is the "target audience" of a short-term mission's service project? Is it a host church? Many projects support a congregation. Such projects may include improvements to a host church's facilities, training or professional development for pastors or staff, and so on. Such initiatives make a visible difference in the life of that host congregation, but usually have a limited impact on the larger community and do not directly address poverty. Some short-term mission projects cast a slightly wider net, benefiting a congregation through offering services—construction assistance, direct aid, whether financial or through donations of clothing or other goods, medical care—to members of that congregation. Is it the community of the host church? In Sabaneta, for example, the goal is to support the local congregation in their outreach to the community, particularly through the medical clinic that serves members of the local population regardless of religious affiliation.

Development professionals often not only think of "target" beneficiaries of a project, but also look at what are usually termed "stakeholders," groups and individuals with an interest in an outcome and the ability to influence that outcome in some way. Stakeholders can advance or complicate both the planning and the implementation of a project. Too narrow a focus on beneficiaries, ignoring other stakeholders, can jeopardize the success of a project. In one community I worked in, for example, a nonprofit organization decided to create a child-feeding center in order to combat the issue of early child-hood malnutrition, which was a significant problem in the rural community they served. The organization obtained funding, rented a building, hired two local women to cook, and opened its doors. The organizers were disap-pointed and frustrated when, after several months, attendance at the free lunches was very low and levels of childhood malnutrition remained virtually unchanged. How was it, staff wondered, that families were not feeding their young children even when the food was free? After much discussion, it was clear that they had been focusing on the beneficiaries—children under the age of five—and ignoring a key stakeholder—the children's mothers. The organization staff had made the assumption that malnutrition was a result of inadequate resources in the household, and that mothers would of course want their children to be better fed. These assumptions were not incorrect—mothers and fathers were deeply concerned about their little ones and made daily choices about how to feed the entire family when there wasn't really enough to go around. But women in the community with small children still didn't bring them to the feeding center for lunch.

After a closer analysis, it became apparent why. In this rural community, most families lived on widely dispersed farms, with many living an hour or more walking distance from the center of the village where the feeding program was located. For a mother to leave the house in the middle of the day, taking two or three hours from her work to walk a toddler down for lunch, meant that completing her other tasks—including preparing lunch for the rest of the family—would be impossible.[3] In every household, adults were working, and older children either were also doing farm work or were in school, leaving no one to take small children in to be fed. Only those families who lived closest to the village used the center on a regular basis. These issues had not occurred to the project planners, who had not consulted with the villagers on the program's structure. If they had, it might have been possible to come up with a different project design, one that would have had a greater chance of success. In this case, parents were key stakeholders whose needs were not considered, even though they clearly were interested in the successful outcome—better childhood nutrition. In other cases, stake-holders can actively obstruct a project—even something as apparently innoc-uous as providing free care might threaten the business practice of a local doctor, for example. Identifying and working with stakeholders early on in a planning process can greatly enhance a project's likelihood of success.

Another concern for organizers is identifying the scope of a project. De-velopment professionals identify four types of projects based on how wide-spread the effects are intended to be and the ways in which the project relates to the larger context.[4] In a case where there are many unknowns, an experi-mental project may fill the gaps. An *experimental project* may often be subject to changes even while the project is under way. An example of an experimental project would be introducing a new species of goat into a community's breeding stock to see how it fares under specific local conditions. A *pilot project* takes an activity that has been done before and applies it in a new location or context, usually starting at a small scale, with the goal of eventually building on a successful project. An example might be to create an afterschool program for teens in an urban neighborhood that lacked activities for adolescents, starting with a small number of teens and increasing that number over time. When a group visits an area repeatedly over a number of years, they can work with local partners to "try out" programs—essentially to run a pilot project, see how it works, and decide whether to pursue a new direction. A third project type is a *demonstration project* in which an example is created so that local people can examine how something works and decide whether to try it themselves. These types of projects are common in agriculture, where perhaps one or two local farmers plant a new crop and invite their neighbors to learn how to cultivate it and see whether it can be successful. A final type, a *production project*, has a well-defined benefit, is already desired or accepted by the community, and is implemented with a goal of generating it as widely as possible. An example might be introducing water filters into a region that has an unreliable drinking water supply, with the goal of distributing filters to every household.

These kinds of projects are developed in phases: framing and planning, implementation and management, and assessment. The initial planning phase lays the groundwork. The implementation phase is when the project is under way and work is actually done. The assessment phase, which is the most often neglected, is a time to reflect on whether the project met its goals, how it could be or could have been improved, and what should happen next.

Planning

Planning projects begins with thinking about goals and objectives. This includes identifying not only the problem, but also why the problem exists. As stakeholders are identified and a planning team is created, the input of these local stakeholders can be essential, beginning with asking what problems they see and how they understand the causes. In this discussion, sensitivity to cultural differences is important, especially when cultural insiders' and outsiders' views of problems and solutions are different. I witnessed one project in the Andes, for example, in which outsiders wanted to curtail teen pregnancy in a community where it was fairly common for unmarried girls of fifteen or sixteen to have babies. In the local culture, however, teens and their parents did not see young mothers as a problem, and teens who became pregnant were not stigmatized. The project, designed as a public education campaign that suggested that teen pregnancy limited girls' life choices, fell flat in a region where most girls—and boys—finished school at age twelve.

Parents felt that having a child would keep their daughter from moving to the city—seen as a dangerous place—to find work as a domestic servant or to the south as a migrant farm laborer, seen as even more hazardous for young women. Projects that seek to solve a "problem" that locals do not see as a problem are rarely successful, and planners may need to reframe the issue, back up a step and address issues of public education, or change approaches. Similarly, if outsiders try to address an issue in ways that beneficiaries do not see as effective, projects will rarely work.

Once planners have thought about a problem and its causes, a key step is to identify leverage points, thinking about what changes will have the greatest impact. In the region around Sabaneta, for example, prostitution is a significant problem, recognized as such by both outsiders and locals. The causes are complex, but it is at least partly due to the presence of many foreign tourists, local poverty, and the lack of employment options for women. Eliminating the tourist industry is clearly not an option, because tourism does bring significant economic benefits to the area, and the elimination of local poverty is surely too ambitious for a service project. A leverage point, then, might be thinking about women's employment options and ways in which that could be addressed. A group seeking to work on this issue might think about what positive and negative influences are already in place and ways in which positive features can be enhanced or introduced, while negative forces are reduced or eliminated. Once a problem and possible causes have been identified, a project can be designed to meet those needs by building on the community's strengths and resources, and many different options can be identified at this point. This hypothetical group could, for example, establish a scholarship program directed at girls and young women, begin a youth program for girls aimed at health education and boosting self-esteem, or create an employment training program for women. They could choose to address the problem in other ways, by lobbying the government to pass and enforce antiprostitution laws, for example. They might decide to work directly with women in the sex trade, providing services that would improve their lives, offering education and job training to provide them with alternative employment, or promoting community organization in order to empower the women themselves.

From these possible alternative approaches, project strategies can be defined. Projects require resources—personnel, materials, space—some of which might already be available and others of which might need to be obtained. In order to be successful, the project has to be matched to the available resources so it can actually be implemented. A given objective can usually be reached in several ways; there is not just one way to solve a problem. In deciding which alternative to choose, planners might think about available personnel and their strengths, interests, and resources. As this basic framework for a project develops, plans for the project can be developed in

more detail. The activities of the project can be defined, along with a deter-
mination of which individuals or organizations are responsible for each project activity.

Throughout the planning stage, a few questions may be helpful for leaders
to consider. First, is the project sustainable over time? What resources will be
required on an ongoing basis? When I lived in northern Argentina, the landscape was littered with the carcasses of old development projects: a windmill
that had been built to generate electricity, with a broken gear that could not
be replaced; a water filtration system whose filters were clogged, and no one
knew how to clean them; a dozen sewing machines, without money to train
local people how to use them; an expensive water desalinization plant that no
one was sure whose responsibility it was to operate, so it sat idle. Without a
clear plan for the future, well-meaning and useful projects can fail to live up
to their potential. A second question to consider at the outset is about the
obstacles to the project. To the extent that these can be anticipated, is it
possible to avoid them or work around them? Here again, thinking about
stakeholders and working with them to make sure their concerns are addressed helps a project run more smoothly. A final set of questions is about
how the project will meet its goals and what its impact will be. Projects often
have unintended consequences, and while these cannot always be anticipated, thinking through how a project could affect different groups and whether
it is appropriate to the cultural context can be helpful. Thinking about a
project's goals and outcomes sets the stage to look to the future.

Implementation

As a project moves from the planning stage to actual implementation, planners are often involved in a whirlwind of details—making sure that things
happen, the logistics of getting people and materials to the right places are
worked out, volunteers are usefully occupied, and services are delivered. In
this phase of a project, stepping back from time to time and evaluating how
things are going can be helpful. Decisions often still have to be made, and
different people will be responsible for making different kinds of decisions.
The decision-making process can be a point where cultural differences once
again come into play. The "right" way to make a decision depends on this
cultural context. In Sabaneta, for example, any significant decisions that the
American team makes are approved by the Dominican pastor. This happens
partly because of the nature of the partnership: The Americans are mindful
that they do not want to make unilateral decisions or take control of the
projects. And it happens partly because of the expectations of Dominican
culture about the role of leaders and the nature of authority in that context. A
development project brings together people with different backgrounds and
cultures who may have varying expectations about participation and decision

making. An awareness of these differences can help to facilitate discussion, make sure that everyone's voice is heard, and result in decisions that are made in ways that are respectful of participants' varying concerns. Projects are most successful when they incorporate local knowledge and expertise and remain respectful of culture and cultural differences.

Assessment

Every project—good or bad—comes to an end, or at least to a pause, which is a good point to assess how things worked and whether the project has met—or approached—its goals. A basic starting point is to see whether the project accomplished what it was supposed to accomplish. This can usually be done using straightforward measures: floors installed, patients seen, filters distributed, and so on. This kind of accounting is often critical to report back to a project's financial supporters, whether members of a home congregation or foundations that provided a grant. This kind of assessment is easier when data are collected on an ongoing basis as the project is being carried out. Knowing whether a project met its goals, exceeded them, or fell short helps in planning the next project.

From a broader perspective, organizers may want to consider whether the project "worked" to meet larger goals. This is a more challenging discussion, particularly because it can be more difficult to measure, especially in the short term. Assessment in development work, as in many fields, tends to focus on what is easiest to measure, but some results are more difficult to quantify. A project may succeed in its shorter-term goals but still fail to produce the desired outcome. A community garden project, for example, could provide some produce to families but not eliminate malnutrition. Or, a project's ultimate outcomes may become apparent only much later, and only by taking a broader perspective. The benefits of an early childhood education center, for example, might not be apparent until those preschoolers finish high school. The ways in which people interact with one another, learn life lessons, offer and accept a helping hand when it is most needed, begin and sustain a friendship may be the most significant, and least measurable, results. Observing and describing these more complex results, in addition to results that can be counted and measured more simply, can remind the planners and supporters of a project of the human dimension of development—which is, after all, at the center of such efforts.

SOCIAL CAPITAL

One result that is difficult to measure is the way in which development programs can foster social ties between individuals and within communities.[5] In times of trouble (such as illness, job loss, or accident) or in times of transition (such as a marriage, a new baby, or the loss of a loved one), people often turn to those around them for help. They may borrow money from a neighbor, accept the offer of a friend to watch the children, or ask an acquaintance for a new job. These informal systems of support are built on relationships of trust and reciprocity and represent a potentially important resource for people in every society.

The concept of social capital describes this "wealth" of community ties—ways in which people in a community feel connected to one another, know one another, and help one another in different situations.[6] Just like financial capital, social capital is a resource, one that people create within communities by participating in different social groups. Researchers have argued that social capital is a powerful resource that increases wealth and productivity, enables democratic government, and supports individual well-being.[7] Although some researchers have used an approach of trying to "measure" social capital, it may be more helpful as a concept that brings attention to intangible yet powerful social ties.

Social capital grows when people are interconnected—through things like civic associations, neighborhood groups, and even bowling leagues. Churches and congregations have long been institutions that produce social capital, bringing people together for a common purpose.[8] John Dilulio, who served as the director of the Office of Faith Based Initiatives during the George W. Bush administration, suggests that in the United States, religious institutions are the most important source of social capital, with a strong tradition of reaching out not just to their own members but also to others around them.[9] Some research has suggested that religious institutions are more effective than other kinds of social institutions at creating connections between people of different classes and socioeconomic groups.[10]

A partnership model can be thought of as a way to build social capital. With the Sabaneta partnership, social capital is developed in two ways. First, the trips bring together individuals who would not otherwise have met—the American visitors and their Dominican hosts. Sonia Patterson is an NGO professional who serves as the lead interpreter for the Pennsylvania group and has traveled to the Dominican Republic dozens of times, both with the team on its annual visit and on her own. Describing the project to a new team member one night at dinner, she said: "The vision is that of a long term, life-long partnership. I see the people here as my extended family, and I mean that." Sonia's feeling of extended family mirrors how many individuals with strong ties to a congregation describe those relationships. Trust within a congregation is like trust within a family, based on an idea of "goodness," shared values, and shared membership.[11] The ties between the American congregations and their Dominican partners resemble those that are created within a single congregation; even though the communities are geographically removed from each other, individuals within them are connected to one another. Another participant contrasted the Sabaneta partnership to short-term missions in which a group travels a single time to a location: "I went once before on a mission trip. The [host community] appreciated the physical labor that got done, but there was no trust. Here [in Sabaneta], you see more of the results of your support."

A second framework for understanding social capital in Sabaneta is that the partnership enhances the role that the IED congregation plays in its local community. Ralph Hawkins, the New Wilmington minister, referred to this process when he reminded team members that their goal for the week's visit was "to help our Dominican brothers and sisters help their neighbors. It is not about us—it is about helping them to do their ministry." Much as U.S. congregations have historically acted as centers for civic engagement, providers of social services, and foundations of communities, providing a basis for the development of social capital, the IED congregation in Sabaneta is positioned to act in the same way. Like members of American congregations, IED church members also take on responsibilities in other civic organizations, volunteering as members of local civil defense, which provides a kind of "neighborhood watch" as well as assisting the police during local events and fiestas and in the public school. Pastor Cancu, who leads the Dominican church, defines social outreach as central to his congregation's role:

> We have to remember that Jesus Christ walked among the poor. Now it is our turn to do so. . . . The church has to get out of its four walls, and has to go outside to the street. We cannot just go to church on Sunday and pray and forget about the people.

Of course, the congregation could, and certainly does, do this without external aid, but it is able to significantly extend its reach with the support of its partners. Speaking to the Americans one night at dinner, Pastor Cancu said:

> There is something I would like you to know. During each visit to Sabaneta de Yásica, you make a big investment in this community. [You spend money] at the hardware store, the supermarket, the pharmacy. [You employ] the people who help with construction, with transportation. Due to the projects you work on, over fifteen professional educators have now graduated from the school and gone on. There are two doctors. There is the school building. There has been progress in health and in education. When people walk by the church, they see Pennsylvania. The community is in motion while you are here. Your work has multiplied the resources that are here.

Although Cancu focused on a few specific examples of how the partnership enhances the local community, it would be easy to point to others, especially the role of the IED in providing social services, including medical care and education. The support of the American partners and the resources they provide have been leveraged, as social capital, in the work of the IED in the community.

"DOING WITH"

Aid professionals and theorists recognize that development should not be "doing to" or "doing for" but "doing with"—that development should not be a process imposed from the outside but should incorporate the desires and perspectives of those it seeks to benefit. This was not always the case. Until the late 1980s, the prevailing model for any development project was to bring in outside professional experts who created a program, implemented it, and left. Decision making was seen as the prerogative of experts and officials. To the extent that local people did not support a project, they were seen merely as obstacles to the process. It is little wonder that so many of these projects failed to meet their own goals and that even more failed to "solve" the problems of poverty. Fortunately, thinking has shifted. Now, the notion that local people should participate in every aspect of a development project is widely accepted in the field.

Participation begins with project planning—defining local issues and making decisions about the best approaches to deal with them. It continues with implementation, with local individuals contributing to make a project work. This can take a number of different forms. Sometimes users of a program are asked to pay a small amount for a service, even if the amount is more symbolic than substantial. Often, contributions may be "in kind," providing labor to install an irrigation system, for example, or contributing food for meetings or for workers. The rationale for requiring participants to contribute is based on two things: first, if a project is desired, people are usually willing to contribute to it in some way, and so the contributions actually demonstrate that community buy-in does exist. Second, once someone has already contributed to a project, he or she is invested in it and is more likely to see it through. Assessment, too, can include local participation and "debriefing," thinking about whether a project succeeded in meeting local needs, what could be done differently, and what else is needed. In each stage, outside experts provide technical assistance and specific knowledge or skills, acting more as consultants than as managers.

The need for development projects to be locally controlled may seem self-evident on the face of it, but making this shift requires a number of changes that can be challenging. It transforms the roles of outside agencies, organizations, and development experts—as well as others, like short-term mission groups, who want to think seriously about transforming conditions of poverty. In the past, these agencies "did" development—arriving with a project that was essentially self-contained, needing locals only as people to do something "to." Similarly, some short-term mission trips, unfortunately, see their destination as interchangeable with any other, looking for "the poor."

Supporting projects that are locally controlled transforms development agencies and their personnel, or short-term mission volunteers, into facilitators—helping a community to organize around an issue or set of issues, formulating a project in ways that make sense to outsiders who may provide financial and other support, obtaining resources, and providing technical support and advice. Outside organizations often play an essential role as intermediaries, bringing material and technical resources to those who need them. Poor communities often lack not just resources but also the skills and networks that are necessary to try to bring in more resources. Outside organizations may be in a better position to mobilize external support and resources. Another role that outside organizations can play is to act as a mediator between different people and groups within a community. People in any community, of course, do not speak with a single voice or share the same opinions, as I will discuss below. These different perspectives need to be taken into account, and outside agencies may be well placed to do this.

Outside experts and volunteers can be challenged by the need to trust in the ability of people who are poor to define their own needs and to make their own decisions. Educated professionals with extensive experience often assume that they can see what the problems are and what the solutions could be—and they can be taken aback when local folks express other priorities. A process that is centered on local decision making does not mean that "experts" should not express opinions or provide advice, but it does mean trying to accept that those opinions are not always "right." The best projects should meet people's needs as they themselves understand them and have clear benefits to them.

Local control over processes of economic development is essential. On a pragmatic level, it makes projects more likely to "work," a case that can perhaps best be illustrated through negative examples. A project that local people do not want, or that does not meet their needs, is likely to fail. I was in a village in the Andes, for example, where a group of engineers from a North American university had recently installed in several households a new type of oven intended to replace the traditional clay ovens that women used. Though the new ovens burned wood, which was scarce in the high elevation villages, they burned less fuel, kept a hotter internal temperature, and produced less smoke. A year later, these new, efficient ovens sat unused. When I asked a woman I was visiting why, she shrugged and told me that the new oven burned the bread and made the kitchen too cold. She never saw the need for it, she continued, and preferred her old oven. The project, the benefits of which seemed self-evident to the engineers, did not consider local needs and priorities. More ominously, projects that do not include local decision making can be detrimental to poor people, making them more vulnerable to poverty, something that is readily evident in larger-scale projects, like road building, mining, or the development of commercial resources. These can undermine traditional access to productive resources like land or forests and undercut local economies.

On a more philosophical level, it seems that accepting local control over projects respects individuals, their communities, and their cultures. Accepting local people's knowledge of their circumstances and their own understandings of their challenges is a way of honoring their dignity and autonomy. "Working with," rather than "doing to," is an expression of humility and grace that recognizes and values human worth. I have often seen faith-based organizations very easily come to this understanding, sometimes more readily than their counterparts in secular agencies. The best short-term mission projects reflect on their relationships with their host communities, incorporate local decision making, and accept local control.

MULTIPLE VOICES

As mentioned above, within any community, people have divergent views and opinions, often in competition or even conflict. Negotiating these divisions can be difficult for project organizers. Good planning, taking into account different stakeholders' perspectives and interests, can mitigate, or at least anticipate, the rise of tension among these different groups. Project planners have learned to seek out likely or possible groups whose interests may differ from another's interests. In the later 1970s, for example, development experts realized that women's interests and opinions were sometimes different from men's. Prior to that time, planners often dealt only with men or with "households" represented by the male partner. But both within the household and within communities, women's interests and focus might be distinct from those of men. Now, projects that fail to account for the perspectives of both men and women are rare. In many communities, ethnic divisions can also represent significant differences that planners need to consider. For faith-based organizations in particular, religious affiliation within a community may represent an important difference that can play a significant role.

I encountered this situation in one of the communities in which I worked in Argentina, which was predominantly Catholic but had a large Protestant minority. The community was nestled in a narrow valley in the Andes. I attended a community meeting that had been set up by an employee of a Catholic aid agency to respond to some problems in the community's child nutrition program—the same kind of program discussed above, but this village was smaller and less physically dispersed. The small room the meeting was held in, usually the setting for the preschool, was filled with women with babies wrapped snugly in ponchos on their backs and toddlers in tow. Some settled themselves on low chairs—not the cheerful child-sized seats that you might find in a North American preschool, but chairs handmade of wood and cowhide, with short legs. Found in every household, they provide a seat that allows easy access to work—shelling beans, tending a fire, weaving—on the ground. When the chairs were full, the remaining women stood around the edges of the room. Most were young or middle-aged mothers, some with as many as eight or ten children. They sat or stood quietly, as did their young children, waiting for the meeting to start.

When the aid worker walked in, she greeted many of the women by name. Three of them were employed by the charity organization to prepare a meal at noon, every day during the week, for young children in the community. After the children were fed, the women would play with them, often teaching songs or letters of the alphabet. The aid worker, Lucia, had earlier explained the program to me this way:

> There are a lot of health problems here. Malnutrition is very bad, especially for children and babies. People have food here, but they really have very little. Most people only eat once a day, maybe, and they might have a soup or a stew, which is mostly liquid. Then they might have some tea with a little bread, and that's it until the next day. The children especially don't get enough to eat. So we have the food program.

The preschool component received less emphasis, by both the charity and the mothers, than the free lunch.

Although the child-feeding program was valued by both community families and the agency that administered it, there was conflict over how it should be run. As Lucia surveyed the room, I knew she was expecting some of this conflict to surface that day. Usually, this meeting for the feeding program was a small affair, a kind of staff meeting for the employees and a couple of the mothers who were most engaged in the preschool. But today the room was full. Lucia was aware that there was some dissatisfaction in the community about the program because she was trying to be stricter about the distribution of food. She had told me: "It's hard to get the women to prepare things properly and then to give it to the infants. No matter how many times we tell them that what we are giving them is for the children, they eat it themselves. They are so hungry themselves that they give the baby one bite, and then they eat six, and it goes like that, so the children aren't getting enough nutrition." When a meal had to be stretched, families often tried to ensure that men and older children had enough to eat after long days spent working in the fields, leaving less for small children. Although sympathetic to the needs of the hungry mothers, she was also mindful of her limited budget and the specific goals of the program to ameliorate child malnutrition.

As the meeting progressed, however, the issue that had drawn out so many women developed somewhat differently. One of the women in the back rose, arms folded across her chest, and agreed with Lucia that resources were indeed scarce. She proposed a solution—to close one of the other child-feeding centers, located in a village across the river. It was unnecessary, she explained as many of her neighbors nodded. Closing it, she continued, would allow the children at this center to continue to receive care. Lucia, taken by surprise by this suggestion, noted that the other center was well attended and that there were many times during the year when the river was impassable, which was why a center had been located there in the first place. As the women looked on disapprovingly, Lucia stated that she would not support closing the other center and that she was sure the women and the organization could work together to find other solutions. She drew the meeting to a rather abrupt close, and the women, although clearly displeased, dutifully filed out.

As a relative newcomer to the community, I was unclear about what had just happened. The organization that Lucia worked for was usually sensitive to responding to and accommodating community requests. Her flat refusal to consider the women's suggestion was atypical and took me by surprise. As I started to ask her about it, she grew visibly angry. "They want to close that center because the families over there don't go to the same church! That is the kind of tension between them. They don't want to feed *those* children. Well, we will feed all of them. They are all God's children!" In this case, she had to decide which set of voices and interests to respond to. Despite the negative consequences in the community, the organization stood by this decision, reaching across the denominational divide to continue to provide services.

The tension between the two villages that Lucia referred to was a difficult issue in the community. One village had largely converted to Protestantism, and residents attended a Baptist church that had been founded by foreign missionaries. The other village, just across the river, had maintained its allegiance to Catholicism—also, of course, introduced by foreign missionaries but much longer ago. Religious differences had split families; I had met brothers who no longer spoke to each other, bitterly divided over their faith. A couple of families who had lived on the "wrong side" of the river—either Catholic or Protestant—had actually moved, resettling on the other side in order to maintain both their religious and their social relations. Perhaps this profound division should not have surprised me. My grandparents had often recounted how they had not been able to adopt a child in the 1940s because both Protestant and Catholic agencies excluded them due to their own "mixed marriage." The contemporary United States certainly continues to have divides—often profound ones—between people and communities of different faiths. Yet we more often consider our more fundamental division to be that between the religious and the secular. And in the United States, as in Argentina and elsewhere, many individuals and organizations actively work to bridge those divides.

In this particular situation, Lucia's position was ultimately vindicated. From my perspective, certainly she did the right thing in maintaining that all of the children in the community deserved to be welcomed into the feeding center. Infant and child malnutrition in the community was a serious problem and one that did not stop at any denominational line. My research on economic conditions in the region did not find any significant differences in rates of poverty and wealth between the majority Catholic residents and their Protestant counterparts. Lucia took a principled moral stand in her assertion that the program was there for everyone, without discrimination, and the organization, sponsored by the Catholic Church, backed up her decision.

There were positive outcomes at the level of the community. The people who were served by the center in the Protestant village felt that their needs were understood, and they certainly felt less animosity, if not toward their neighbors, then toward the Catholic Church itself. The organization and its workers were perceived, in this situation and in others, as neutral and equitable advocates for the entire community. Although some of the women left Lucia's meeting feeling disgruntled, it did not cause any lasting friction. In fact, a woman who was not at the meeting but was part of the church community commented to me later that it was a good lesson in loving one's neighbor.

The tensions evident in this example, between Catholic and Protestant, are not uncommon throughout Latin America. Most Protestants in Latin America are recent converts, the result of a number of converging trends. In the second half of the twentieth century, most of the nations of Central and South America moved from giving the Catholic Church official and in some cases nearly exclusive official status to being officially secular or religiously plural. This change allowed the growth of other faiths, which was in some cases rapid. The majority of Protestants, then, are recent converts. Both Catholics and Protestants tend to draw sharp, and as we have seen, sometimes divisive lines between members of each faith. Many Protestant converts, in the process of religious conversion, reject not just their prior religion, but also social and cultural norms, shunning drinking, gambling, and other behaviors, often creating a high degree of community tension. In the Andean village I lived in, recent converts rejected many social traditions that were associated not just with religious faith but also with the indigenous culture of the highlands. This rejection, rather than differences in religious doctrine or practice, caused the deepest rifts in families and the broader community, as families encountered conflict in celebrating holidays, ceremonies, and even events like weddings and birthdays together. Some scholars believe that in time, families and communities will be able to negotiate these divisions more

successfully, as increasing numbers of non-Catholics are born into their faith
traditions and perhaps will feel less of a need to vehemently reject other,
especially nonreligious, practices to assert their distinctions. In the mean-
time, however, this is an example of one kind of conflict within a community
that an outside organization may be faced with. In such circumstances, organizations or groups may need to clarify whether they will focus on just one
part of the population or transcend internal divisions. As with any other
issue, the decision may depend on circumstances and on the nature of the
work that is being done, but external organizations can play an important role
in negotiating differences and building models of trust and cooperation that
can begin to transcend local divisions.

GETTING THINGS DONE

Being of service to others is an essential part of short-term missions. And in
this service, mission participants find tremendous personal rewards. Yet they
also strive to genuinely be *of service*—to help those in need. Creating and
sustaining effective development projects—ones that offer charity when that
is essential, create development when that is possible, and support social
justice as an expression of our aspirations for others and the world we
share—is the way to make this service most meaningful not just to those who
volunteer, but also to those with whom they work.

Planning and implementing meaningful projects, projects that make a
difference in people's lives, can seem like a daunting task. Short-term missions entail a substantial investment of time, energy, goodwill, and financial
resources. Good stewardship includes the responsibility to spend these resources wisely. Many short-term mission projects unfortunately engage volunteers in tasks that do not ultimately make good use of resources, requiring
menial labor that keeps them busy but does not enrich the lives of those they
seek to serve. But other mission groups find ways to engage in service that
contributes in some way to alleviating issues of poverty. Investing in meaningful work is ultimately more satisfying for volunteers, who can then feel
that they have made a substantial contribution to the well-being of others.

Although "efficiency" in creating economic change is not a primary goal,
or even a concern of short-term mission experiences, service is not made
more genuine by being inefficient. In working against poverty, good inten-
tions are no substitute for planning and effective action.[12] By learning from
NGOs and other organizations with long histories of development work,
short-term mission projects can direct their substantial efforts in directions
that do make a difference.

NOTES

1. Michael Taylor. *Not Angels but Agencies: The Ecumenical Response to Poverty—A Primer.* Geneva: WCC Publications, 1995, 144.

2. Riall Nolan. *Development Anthropology: Encounters in the Real World.* Boulder, CO: Westview Press, 2001.

3. The program also offered meals to women who were pregnant or breastfeeding, as mothers' nutrition during pregnancy and lactation is essential to infant health and nutrition. In fact, most of the women who did regularly bring preschoolers and toddlers to the program were pregnant or nursing and were provided with their own lunch along with their children's.

4. Nolan.

5. Some sociologists have devised systems to measure or quantify social capital. The growing technique of Social Network analysis offers powerful analytic tools to examine social networks and social capital.

6. Robert D. Putnam. "Bowling alone: America's declining social capital." *Journal of Democracy* 6 (1995): 65–78.

7. For example, see ibid.

8. It may be worth noting here that although sociologists and others studying the social aspects of religion find this concept to be useful analytically, the missional church movement offers a criticism that the "citizenship" role of congregations may distract or detract from a more clearly defined religious focus. See Darrell L. Guder, ed. *Missional Church: A Vision for the Sending of the Church in North America.* Grand Rapids, MI: Eerdmans, 1998, 78, 108–109.

9. John J. Dilulio. *Godly Republic: A Centrist Blueprint for America's Faith-Based Future.* Berkeley: University of California Press, 2007, 20.

10. Robert D. Putnam and David E. Campbell. *American Grace: How Religion Divides and Unites Us.* New York: Simon and Schuster, 2010, 253–254.

11. Robert Wuthnow. *Saving America? Faith-Based Service and the Future of Civil Society.* Princeton, NJ: Princeton University Press, 2004, 243–247.

12. Krista Tippett. *Speaking of Faith: Why Religion Matters—and How to Talk about It.* New York: Penguin, 2007, 113.

Chapter Six

Seeing the Big Picture

When I began this research, as a researcher who has focused on antipoverty organizations for years, I was skeptical about the ability of short-term missions to make any substantial difference in the lives of poor communities. So much money is being spent, I figured, on travel expenses for relatively wealthy North Americans journeying to provide volunteer labor in regions that have no shortage of unemployed laborers. In some cases, such as construction, local people may be more skilled than the Americans who come to "help." Why not just pay local people to do that work? From my vantage point, it seemed as though the short-term mission model was an inefficient approach, at best. Why not just send a check? I wondered. As my research developed further, I came to understand that participants see "sending a check" as an inadequate response to the problems of poverty. Some have concerns, as one participant expressed to me, that recipients "don't know what to do with it," that money sent as aid will not be productive but will be squandered or put to frivolous uses. But more commonly, the participants whom I spoke to are motivated by the desire to build a genuine connection, a relationship, with those in need. For them, "just" sending a check feels too impersonal, too anonymous. It does not convey the same sense of touching the lives of others in a meaningful way.

As I began to talk to more people involved in short-term missions, I found that they genuinely did want to help. They do not expect to transform the world, but they do hope that they can have an impact on someone's life. They often hope, and sometimes find, that this changes their own lives, allowing them to see themselves and their own circumstances from a new vantage point. As I have reflected more on short-term mission, I have come to believe that it provides a way for American participants to understand poverty, to understand their own culture, and to begin to think about framing relationships that bridge divides of class and geography. And it has the potential to make a material difference in the lives of the host communities that the Americans visit.

Participants and leaders have many goals for the short-term mission experience—personal growth, spiritual development, enhanced cross-cultural understanding, and the alleviation of poverty. They want to know the people they are helping. Participants want the time and money that they spend to be effective, and they want to invest not just their money, but also their sense of self, their heart, and their compassion. As one participant told me:

> People at our home church would ask, how much of the money that you spent traveling could go back into our community? But seeing people here [in Sabaneta]—I am getting an education by coming here. It's very concrete. Here's where my money went, a kid moved up a grade. It's different from the U.S., where the issues seem much more complex. Here, there is so much poverty that even a little helps so much.

Creating and maintaining aid projects is an essential component of successful short-term missions. They do channel significant resources into poorer communities, and these resources should be mobilized as effectively as they can be. But as my own understanding of the short-term mission phenomenon grew, I came to believe that the experience of service that participants find in short-term mission is also important, for personal growth and for transforming the ways in which participants see themselves. They can gain a greater sensitivity to and appreciation of cultural differences. They can develop a greater understanding of the challenges of poverty and the conditions that can make the lives of those who are poor better or worse. They can begin to see themselves and their choices as interrelated with the lives of others.

My initial skepticism has turned to a qualified endorsement. Short-term mission has the potential to engage participants in issues of poverty, to raise awareness in individuals who might otherwise not be exposed to global problems, and to transform the ways in which Americans understand people in other cultures. It can mobilize resources that would not otherwise be available for charity, development, and social justice. It represents an outpouring of compassion and generosity that reaffirms my optimism about the human condition. I say my endorsement is "qualified," however, because short-term mission does not always do these things. If the service undertaken as part of short-term mission is only a gesture, without making a real difference to those who are poor, then it is an illusion, one that merely assuages the guilt of the privileged. The potential of short-term mission to alleviate poverty and inequality depends on the individuals and organizations involved. Fortunately, good models are available, based on experience and scholarly research, that can make short-term mission more likely to be effective in meeting the multiple goals of individuals, congregations, communities, and organizations.

BEST PRACTICES FOR SHORT-TERM MISSION

After several years of talking to short-term mission participants, reading scholarly accounts of the short-term mission phenomenon, reviewing numerous writings by religious leaders in short-term missions, and going on mission trips myself, I realize that in mission, like in economic development, there is no single "right" way. What works depends very much on the goals of congregations and participants, the strengths and concerns of host communities, and the context of each mission group and each trip. That said, some conditions and practices seem to support better mission trips, ones that contribute more to alleviating conditions of poverty and to creating genuine relationships between communities.

Establish Long-Term Relationships

Although short-term mission is, by its very definition, limited in duration, it is most effective in the context of a long-term relationship. This can be achieved in a number of different ways—through a direct partnership between congregations or a sister-parish arrangement; by working with a faith-based or nongovernmental organization with a long-term presence in a community; through one-time participation in a longer-term denominational program that links congregations globally. Even in the case of a natural disaster or other emergency, when a congregation may feel called to send aid and volunteers to a region in which it does not have any existing relationships, this aid is much more effective if it is offered through an existing organization with an established presence "on the ground." Without a long-term commitment, short-term mission is a kind of religious tourism—useful, interesting, and maybe even transformational for those who go, but not making a significant impact on the community that hosts them.

Development projects are most successful when organizers understand the local culture and community and when that community has significant, meaningful input into projects. A long-term relationship improves the likelihood of both of these conditions. That allows resources—volunteers, materials, financial support—to be deployed more successfully. It means that a short-term mission trip can be part of a long-term investment, developing social capital and sustaining specific projects over a long period of time. In Sabaneta, for example, team members who have been participating over many years see that their efforts have had a long-term impact. One of the doctors offered her assessment, saying:

> Now, when we go we can get some education done. That is changing what
> happens over the long term. It isn't about just putting on Band-Aids. We can
> work to fill in the gaps in the [local] system, and give it a boost. If you define
> success by improving the reputation of the public health system, we have been
> 100 percent successful.

By developing a relationship with the public clinic over many years, the
American team contributed to a meaningful, long-term improvement in the
quality of life in the Sabaneta community.

Choosing a location, going back repeatedly, and allowing a relationship
to develop and grow is a way for short-term mission groups to make the
biggest impact and has additional practical benefits as well. Working through
a long-term partner helps to ensure a smooth experience for travelers and
keeps surprises—and the stress of unanticipated circumstances—to a minimum. In Sabaneta, "old-timers" offer practical suggestions for newcomers to
the group. Visiting the same location repeatedly may also make the trip seem
less like a tourist jaunt, an expedition in search of a novel experience and
new sights.

Reflect on the Experience

Researchers and congregational leaders who have been involved in short-
term mission for years agree that mission trips are much more effective, in a
host of different ways, when participants are engaged in examining the purpose of their experience not just during the trip but also before and after the
trip. Orientation and debriefing can help to provide participants with a space
to reflect on their personal and spiritual development, the meanings that the
experience carries for them, and a sense that their involvement in a mission
trip can enrich their "ordinary" life. Typically, groups are more likely to
engage in orientation activities than in posttrip reflection, probably because
of the excitement leading up to a trip and the need to cover logistical planning.

For some participants, reflection on their experiences comes naturally and
is an inevitable part of what they do. Other participants may benefit from a
structure that provides a time for thought and conversation. When I began
interviewing college-aged mission participants, it sometimes seemed to me
that the interview itself served as a space for them to reflect on their experience. The very first young woman whom I interviewed thanked me, which
took me by surprise—I had never been thanked for an interview before. As I
interviewed more mission participants, I found that many of them expressed
gratitude to me—for listening, for understanding, for asking questions. The
themes I have addressed in this book—culture and cultural difference, poverty and inequality, service and responsibility to others—have emerged from
the concerns and reflections of those that I interviewed and traveled with.

Interviews, of course, are not the most common forum for this kind of thoughtful reflection; trip leaders and planners can provide ways for participants to think through their experiences—not just a review of activities or events, but a more substantial reflection on what it means to them.

The opportunity to contextualize the short-term mission experience through reflection before and after an actual trip can be another incentive to conduct a short-term mission within a long-term partnership or stable relationship with a host community or organization. Rather than being a single event, a mission trip becomes a regular part of an annual cycle. Participants can understand the host community not as an exotic, unknown location but as a familiar place. Even a new participant is likely to know someone who has been there before. To the extent that the community that is visited is part of the regular discussions of a congregation throughout the year, not just in the weeks leading up to and following a mission trip, participants and other members of a congregation have an opportunity to engage in reflection and discussion of the issues of the mission.

Serve Others—Through Projects that Make a Difference

The service work that mission participants do is an essential part of their experience and something that many mission participants clearly feel is transformational. It can become an important part of how volunteers see not just others but also themselves in relation to others. But the benefits to the individual are subsumed by the notion, both theologically and practically, that the service itself should be useful and meaningful to those who are served. Channeling service through effective development projects, ones that have proven themselves to make a difference in the lives of people who are economically disadvantaged, puts the time and resources of short-term mission to its best use.

There is no "one-size-fits-all" development project, but several principles outlined in the previous chapter suggest strategies to make service work more beneficial. Most importantly, the best projects begin with planners seeking out and listening to the opinions of host partners in planning and implementing projects. Good projects also happen when planners shift as much control as possible to individuals and groups in the host community. They build on strengths—the strengths of the host community, the skills and talents of volunteer participants, and the resources that are available. Focusing on strengths and available resources shifts the ways in which participants think about a "poor" community, pointing out its advantages rather than simply its deficits. It also can make projects more sustainable, in the sense that they are less reliant solely on outside support. In order to be most effective, outside groups examine charity, development, and social justice and work toward creating projects that address the causes and not just the symptoms.

Understand the Role of Culture

Christian theology has turned in the past several decades toward a more global understanding of religious beliefs and practices, one that is sensitive to the ways in which the Bible and the church are interpreted through different cultural lenses. Theologians recognize and validate these differences in interpretation and learn from one another across cultural differences. Work in economic development, to a lesser degree, has taken the same turn. Development theorists and practitioners place a new emphasis on the significance of local knowledge—people's own understanding of their system of production, their ecology, and their relationships—and the ways this can shape a local economy. Across both of these fields, theorists recognize that no single culture has a monopoly on truth. Rather, our understanding is enhanced through learning from one another.

Both fields also recognize that culture matters. Culture is not just the clothes one wears or the music one listens to, but it refers to more fundamental patterns of thought and behavior through which people understand the world and one another. Short-term mission explicitly creates a framework for interaction between people from different cultures and has become an enormously popular way for Americans to meet people from other cultures. But participants sometimes have a tendency to collapse cultural differences, seeing "the poor" as interchangeable or as homogenous. This tendency is an obstacle to cultural understanding as well as a barrier to the creation of authentic relationships across cultures. Discussing culture and cultural differences is one tool to avoid this pitfall. Investing time to learn about the political, historical, and economic context of the host culture provides participants with a better understanding of the significance of the work they do. Learning the language of the host culture, even at a rudimentary level, can lower barriers and facilitate more interaction. Inviting people from the host culture to address the group, either during orientation "at home" or during the trip itself, can increase understanding. It could also provide a bridge between mission "over there" and mission at home through building connections with immigrant communities in the United States. Some models for short-term mission pair a group from the host country, if not the host community, with a group visiting from abroad, which opens up the cultural dynamic in an interesting way. Cultural understanding is not a luxury, but rather a fundamental part of the success of service and economic development.

Work in Partnership

Our understanding of both "mission" and "development" has come a long way in the past few decades. Although both originated as colonial institutions, in the context of hierarchy and inequality, they both have been reconceptualized as horizontal relationships within a diffuse network of relationships and mutual understanding, learning, and growth. The contemporary ideals for mission and for development are decentralization and a grassroots approach, taking into account cultural differences and local contexts.

The question is not *whether* we travel and work with others; the question is *how*. The concept of global mission, "mission from everywhere, to everywhere," is well established, at least as a goal or model, by many short-term mission groups as they strive to understand their relationships to other communities. In the same way, development projects can also promote control over the process to the people whose lives are most immediately affected. In both cases, those of us from relatively wealthier cultures can learn from others and from their experiences and begin to think about our own conditions and transformations as well as theirs.

TELLING STORIES

In April 2013, I again accompanied the team to Sabaneta. I had promised myself that this year I was going strictly as a "participant," not as a "participant observer," my professional role, but by midway through the week I found myself with my notebook once again in hand, jotting down people's stories. I was reminded that ethnographic research like mine captures an institution, a community, a phenomenon at one specific moment in time. And although research begins and ends, the thing being studied continues: It grows, diminishes, changes. It responds to external circumstances as well as to internal dynamics. I was "officially" done with my research—done with interviews and taking notes—but the partnership, and my engagement with it, is ongoing.

For me, stories are an essential part of what all humans have in common—our need to make sense of external events and our internal responses. We make meaning through stories, giving shape to our circumstances, giving voice to our experiences, and giving value to things that happen to us and to our responses to them. This process of making meaning seems universal across cultures. We all tell stories, although the content and style are wonderfully variable. One of the things I most appreciate about anthropology is its attentiveness to people's stories—not the stories of important people, or celebrities, or those who are somehow prominent, but the stories of ordinary people—farmers and fishers, parents and siblings, the well-to-do and the destitute, individuals in the crowd—recognizing that each is both unique and representative of a cultural whole. Our stories make us feel that we matter, that no matter how small our actions may seem, they are relevant and significant. Short-term mission, for some participants, if not all, serves as an element in a personal narrative, one that allows the individual to create meaning. The mission experience can become a catalyst for reframing the stories of participants and also for reshaping how they think about global poverty.

Short-term mission changes—at least potentially—the stories that participants tell about themselves and about others. Volunteers usually have a story that explains their complex motives for their participation in a mission trip, often related to their religious beliefs and their conceptions of themselves. The act of volunteering and a volunteer's reflection on his or her service create a sense of being not just a *helpful* person but a *good* one. Volunteering becomes a way to connect with an inner, moral sense of self—to see oneself as a fundamentally caring person. As the short-term mission participant immerses him- or herself in an extraordinary act of volunteering, one that involves separation from ordinary life, physical challenges, and personal transformation, this sense of the moral self can become an important part of the story he or she tell about him- or herself. Short-term missions provide an intense opportunity to create stories and re-create our selves, which may be what makes them so much more powerful than simply sending a check, even if they are less financially efficient in terms of their actual impact on poverty.

Short-term mission also provides an opportunity for participants to be attentive to the stories of others. Although other forms of travel also bring Americans in contact with people from other cultures, short-term mission is certainly one of the most popular and may be accessible to a broader range of travelers than other kinds of trips. Mission travel is a way for participants to experience other cultures, but even more, to get to know people from those other cultures. The emphasis on building relationships and connections leads participants to rethink cultural differences, what it means to be wealthy and what it means to be poor, and the ways in which people are connected to one another. A manageable first step in confronting poverty and inequality is to venture out and put human faces and voices to poverty. Our stories come to include these experiences and become stories of conversation and compassion.

For me, a focus on the ways in which people make meaning in their lives is a way of respecting and valuing human dignity, a way of affirming individuals and the cultures they create and inhabit together. Short-term mission, at its best, is also a way of recognizing and appreciating human dignity. Through service, participants find new meaning in their own lives and reflect on their relationships with others. Through the encounter with poverty, they experience the effects of social injustice and inequality. Through developing relationships, they learn the stories of others and gain a perspective on our shared humanity. Their volunteer service is a manifestation of compassion, an act of concern for others, and a way to learn and grow. It has the potential to transform not just those who are served, but also those who serve, in ways that can make a genuine difference in the world.

Suggested Resources

Mission leaders and participants might find the following resources helpful.

BOOKS ON SHORT-TERM MISSION

Howell, Brian. *Short-Term Mission: An Ethnography of Christian Travel Narrative and Experience*. Downers Grove, IL: IVP Academic, 2012.
Aimed at scholars, this book offers sensitive insights into short-term mission using a case study of evangelical college students in the Dominican Republic.

Livermore, David. *Serving with Eyes Wide Open: Doing Short-Term Missions with Cultural Intelligence*. Grand Rapids, MI: Baker Books, 2006.
Livermore focuses on creating cultural sensitivity in and through short-term mission work, from theological and practical perspectives.

Priest, Robert J. *Effective Engagement in Short-Term Missions: Doing It Right!* Pasadena, CA: William Carey Library, 2008.
This book is a collection of articles by scholars and practitioners of short-term mission. It covers topics ranging from mobilizing resources for mission work to cross-cultural understanding, to the impact of short-term missions on college-aged participants.

BOOKS ON ECONOMIC DEVELOPMENT

There are many scholarly works that focus on development in specific areas of the world that might be helpful for mission groups. Here, I am offering a few that take a broader perspective on economic development.

Kidder, Tracy. *Mountains beyond Mountains*. New York: Random House, 2003.
A biography of physician and anthropologist Paul Farmer, this book describes Farmer's work in Haiti and his dedication to transforming conditions of poverty. Readers interested in

Farmer's views might also enjoy the more challenging *Pathologies of Power: Health, Human Rights, and the New War on the Poor*, by Farmer himself (Berkeley: University of California Press, 2003).

Sachs, Jeffrey D. *The End of Poverty: Economic Possibilities for Our Time*. New York: Penguin, 2005.
Sachs, an economist and director of the nonprofit Earth Institute, examines social, economic, political, and environmental issues and suggests holistic solutions.

Sen, Amartya. *Development as Freedom*. New York: Knopf, 1999.
Nobel Prize–winning economist Amartya Sen explains why freedom—the ability to make choices—is the key not just to economic development but also to realizing human potential, in a way that those of us who are not economists can understand.

WEBSITES AND BLOGS

Act Alliance
www.actalliance.org
Act Alliance is a global network of churches and faith-based organizations working against poverty. The website includes news and updates about different programs.

CIA World Factbook
https://cia.gov.library/publications/the-world-factbook
This web page offers easy access to reliable, basic information about every country in the world.

First Third
http://www.firstthird.org/blog/default.aspx?m=3924&post=2477
This blog focuses on youth ministry but includes numerous essays and commentaries on short-term mission.

United Nations Millennium Development Goals
http://www.un.org/millenniumgoals/
In 2000, the United Nations embarked on an ambitious program to end global poverty. The Millennium Development Goals lay out broadly agreed-upon goals, such as reducing child mortality and achieving universal primary education. The web page offers positive models for programs, reports on progress that has been made toward the goals, and links for action.

World Bank Human Development Network
http://web.worldbank.org/wbsite/external/extaboutus/exthdnetwork/0,,menupk:514432~page pk:64158571~piPK:64158630~thesitepk:514426,00.html
As may be evident from the web address, the World Bank doesn't always have the easiest website to navigate, but it does offer a wealth of information about poverty and development issues throughout the world. The World Bank also offers an enormous array of reports and project summaries, which can be accessed online for free (or can be accessed directly at the simpler www.worldbank.org/reference). Some are focused on a specific country or region, while others focus on a topic or issue.

World Faiths Development Dialogue
www.berkleycenter.georgetown.edu/wfdd
This ecumenical organization is a think tank that examines the ways in which religious organizations engage in antipoverty programs and policies.

CPSIA information can be obtained at www.ICGtesting.com
Printed in the USA
BVOW07s2028120714

358947BV00004B/5/P